A Choice of
KEATS'
Verse

Selected

with an introduction by
C. DAY LEWIS

FABER AND FABER

3 Queen Square
London

*First published in 1971
by Faber and Faber Limited
3 Queen Square London WC1
Printed in Great Britain by
R. MacLehose and Company Limited
The University Press Glasgow
All rights reserved*

ISBN 0 571 09555 0

Contents

Acknowledgements

The text of the poems and extracts in the selection follow that of H. W. Garrod's Oxford English Texts edition of *The Poetical Works of John Keats* 2nd edition 1958, by permission of Clarendon Press, Oxford.

Introduction

'Art', a distinguished American critic has recently said, 'is not quite so autonomous as twentieth-century criticism likes to think.' Unlike Wordsworth, for whom he had a great respect though his poetic aims were so different, Keats was at no period of his short life so emotionally caught up in public affairs as Wordsworth had once been. His poetry was untouched by politics as it was untouched by orthodox religion. He was the nearest thing to a 'pure poet' in the England of his time. But this is not to say that his poetry can best be considered in isolation from the events and influences of his life: without the *Letters*, for instance, the finest ever written by an English poet, we should miss vital clues to the quality of his mind — the vivacity, vigour and profound originality of thought which enabled a bookish but unsophisticated young man to lift himself from the meek artificiality of his early work and break through into the larger world of 'Hyperion' and the Odes.

John Keats was born in 1795, son of a livery-stable manager. On his father's death his mother remarried, but died in 1810 leaving Keats, two younger brothers and a sister in the charge of her own mother, Mrs Jennings, and Richard Abbey, the trustee and guardian appointed in their grandfather's will. Abbey, a self-righteous man of doubtful honesty, contrived to keep the bulk of their grandfather's patrimony from the Keats children during the years when they, and John most of all, sorely needed it. The conflict between the demands of his art and his sense of responsibility to the young family would for years perturb the poet's mind.

As a schoolboy at Edmonton, Keats was known for his 'courage, sensitivity and generosity.' He received a grounding in the classics, which was to be reflected from many of his poems. The 'violence and vehemence' of his temperament, the ardent eye and bantam stature, would never be forgotten by his contemporaries. On leaving school, Keats was first apprenticed to an Edmonton surgeon, and then at the age of 20 became a student and a dresser at Guys Hospital. It was there that a fellow-student recalled him 'always at the window, peering into space.' And, as W. J. Bate says of the poet's reading, only seriously begun after leaving school, 'henceforth the open door, the open window, became a haunting metaphor to Keats.'

His first contact in the literary world was with Leigh Hunt. Hunt's verse, as well as his generous encouragement, exercised a strong influence on the younger man. The less admirable lessons he learnt from the verse had in due course to be unlearnt: but in another respect Leigh Hunt's influence was lasting — the emphasis he laid upon the links between poetry and the visual arts. It was a period when a renaissance was thought to be taking place in English art: 'ut pictura, poesis' had intense meaning for Keats; and Ian Jack has shown in his *Keats and the Mirror of Art* how often his poems, both the subjects and the individual images, appear to have had their inception in some print or original work of art Keats studied.

Through Leigh Hunt Keats met the painter, Haydon, from whom he learnt not to be daunted by grandiose conceptions, and presently Hazlitt, whose unorthodox and severe critical judgement would prove a counterweight to Haydon's large enthusiasms. It was the connection with Hunt that laid Keats open to the virulent attacks launched by Blackwoods upon the 'Cockney School' of poets. But Keats was not 'snuffed out' by reviews: his first *Poems* had been kindly treated, when the book was noticed at all; and he had already lost interest and belief in *Endymion* before he had finished it and Lockhart delivered his onslaught.

It is difficult to think of Keats' achievement without feeling there was something unnatural, or preternatural, about its tempo: I feel the same while looking at a film in which the slow growth of a plant is speeded up into a sequence of a few minutes. His life seems a vista of crises, despairs, decisions and departures, all abruptly foreshortened. Visits to Margate, the Isle of Wight, Oxford, Devonshire, Scotland (the last activated in him the tuberculosis which would shortly kill his brother Tom): brother George leaving with his bride for America: the love for Fanny Brawne, desperate only because money was short and health worsening: the voyage to Italy, the last agonies in Rome, the epitaph 'Here lies one whose name was writ in water' — these things pass so rapidly before the mind's eye that they might almost be whipped on by Keats' impetuous and impatient genius.

Knowing how brief his life would be, we are tempted to think he too must have had foreknowledge of early death, even before the first haemorrhage, and that this foreknowledge both heightened the fever of creation and also impelled him to produce in his poetry those characteristic moments of stasis — those time-arresting images (the Grecian Urn is the most famous) which could create for him, as they do for us, an illusion that time may be disarmed and turned into a friend of man. All poets seek to build refuges from the flood. But Keats' urgency was increased by a belief that concerned something larger than the poetic faculty.

When he said in a letter that the world is a 'vale of soul-making', he meant exactly what he said. We come into the world as merely potential beings, acquiring a 'soul' — by which he seems to have meant a sense of identity — through rightly-interpreted experiencing of life. So, one assumes, a long life is desirable for the perfecting of a soul. But against this we have to set Keats' paradox that the poet has no identity (and is therefore 'the most unpoetical of all God's Creatures'). This paradox is a result of Keats' moving through the influences of Spenser, Milton, even Dryden, more and more under the influence of Shakespeare: and Shakespeare above all writers possessed what Keats called 'negative capability' — the power to *lose* one's identity in something outside the self. It was this ideal of disinterestedness, of striving always for a subject outside himself, which enabled Keats to advance so rapidly from the conventional prettiness of his earliest work to the mature beauty of his latest.

I have called him a 'bookish' poet because, although he was virile and of a sufficiently extrovert temper, the inspiration of his verse was literary. If we compared him with a young poet of our own day, we would see how immensely more interested Keats was in the craft of versification, and how he started with highly conventional ideas of the way to set about becoming a poet. It was incumbent on him to attempt a long poem, for instance: so he dashed off on *Endymion* with the avowed intention of 'filling' four thousand lines. On the other hand, he shared with the poet of today the depressing conviction that everything which could be done in poetry has already been done, and far better than we could hope to do it. Keats felt that 'there was nothing original to be written in poetry; its riches were already exhausted — and all its beauties forestalled.'

Originality, which would have been a meaningless concept to a poet a hundred years before, had now taken on a formidable importance for the arts. We could claim for Keats that he was the ancestor of the modern poet in that he showed this self-consciousness about originality which has been a chief characteristic of poetry ever since. Its effect is to reduce poetry to more and more subjective themes. The desire to be different not only tempts the poet into extravagance and eccentricity of style: it also puts a blight on the traditional subjects of poetry.

What was singular in Keats from the start was felicity of phrase — the recognition as well as the mastery of it. When Cowden Clarke and he read from Chapman's translation of the *Odyssey*, his friend caught Keats' 'delighted stare' at the passage ending 'The sea had soak'd his heart through'. Early the next morning he wrote his first great poem — the sonnet whose sestet is an example of his visual imagination and superb gift for phrase-making. This poem went into his first book, together with some fugitive pieces and two longer ones — 'I Stood Tip-toe' and 'Sleep and Poetry'. The first of these captivated me as a schoolboy. Lines like 'A little noiseless noise among the leaves', or 'Here are sweet peas on tip-toe for a flight', or the minnows 'Staying their wavy bodies 'gainst the stream' — the pictures they bring to my senses are still fresh.

Sonnets were to Keats negligible things one wrote to fill in an hour or mark an occasion ('Did our great Poets ever write short pieces?'), and the next book would be *Endymion*, which later he described as 'a feverish attempt, rather than a deed accomplished'. The poem must be seen as a titanic exercise and a 'test of Invention', not judged as a work of art. Keats had not yet learnt — he never learnt except in the Odes and other short poems — to put bone into a work and articulate a coherent poetic argument. Long enough, so he hoped, to give the imagination room to move in, *Endymion* in fact taught Keats the virtues of compression and coherence. Writing the poem must also have made him perceive certain technical points — the danger of feminine rhymes, the impossibility of gaining narrative momentum from the basic metre he had adopted. But, as W. J. Bate says, 'Keats' critical perception keeps leaping ahead of his own poetry.'

The *Lamia* volume, published two years after *Endymion*, shows the giant strides Keats had taken in his art. It contains the five great odes, the first 'Hyperion', and three story-poems. Four of the five odes were written in a few weeks of the spring of 1819: 'To Autumn' in the fall of the same year. And it is worth remembering that their form grew out of Keats' experiments with the sonnet.

'Isabella; or the Pot of Basil', the poem Keats was soon to condemn as 'mawkish', hardly deserves such censure. The plot was taken from Boccaccio, Keats adding to it certain digressions in the Chaucerian manner. There are sentimentalities indeed; but technically, in its use of *ottava rima* for one thing, the poem has a dryness and decisiveness very different from Hunt's verse, while we should find it difficult to use the word 'mawkish' of the poignant and unsparing passage where Isabella finds her murdered lover's head. 'Lamia' I myself find more ambitious but less successful. It is a poem about illusion and reality: the fable itself, taken from the *Anatomy of Melancholy*, decorates and overshadows this theme, rather than illuminating it, while the movement of Keats' imagination does not sit comfortably to the Dryden-influenced diction. Of the three narrative poems, I like best 'The Eve of St. Agnes'. Here Keats gave full play to his sensuousness: the poem luxuriates without inhibition in the colour and detail of the subject, which combines a vaguely mediaeval setting with a pictorial treatment that anticipates the pre-Raphaelites. A dream within a dream, the poem keeps consistently to a right level of seriousness, with no irritable gropings after a philosophy.

It was written after Keats had abandoned the first 'Hyperion', which (with its successor) might be called the greatest failed poem in the English language. Its famous opening lines were poetry at a higher sustained level than Keats had yet achieved. How could its inspiration have died away? Whatever the reason, Keats clearly lost faith in the original conception: the statuesque images, the Miltonic diction did not, I suspect, conceal from him for long a thinness of thought beneath, a falling-short of what was intended — some authoritative utterance on the human condition. But Keats was still a very young man; and when, increasingly ill and desperate, he attempted the theme again in 'The Fall of Hyperion', although a Dantesque approach improved matters, the substance of Canto One is still a dream — and a more personal and inward-directed one than that of the first 'Hyperion'. The colloquy with Moneta, aimed at clarifying and enlarging the poet's values, comes nearer to calling them in question.

The trouble with both Hyperions is probably the same as that which rendered *Endymion* a (much less) magnificent failure — the constant resort to symbolisms either invented to give weight to the theme or used in so idiosyncratic a way that they lose much of collective force which tradition gave them. The fables, being the rootless, have for the reader too much the insubstantial feel of fantasy.

In this respect, as in others, the Odes are triumphant. Even the Nightingale's highest flights of fancy never lose touch with a human situation, a human mood we can recognise and respond to: we do not question the existence of those figures which decorate the Grecian urn, any more than we argue about the physical facts of 'To Autumn'. In these poems illusion and reality join hands and become one. In them Keats brought to a fine pitch all he had learned about poetic technique and emotional truth. For instance, the 'Nightingale', 'Melancholy', and the 'Grecian Urn' make frequent use of contraries — contrasting moods or facets of a theme, not verbal paradoxes to which Keats was unsympathetic. If we wish to become closely acquainted with melancholy, we should not look for her amid the conventional trappings: she is most keenly savoured when set against bright things — a rose, a rainbow, globed paeonies, an angry woman's eyes. Melancholy feeds on such things because she lives in the very heart of beauty and joy, so that only the man who tastes these to the full can fully realise their transience and make an absolute surrender to 'the melancholy fit'.

'Ode to a Nightingale' is a set of variations on a theme which is essentially the contrast between two opposing states of mind — one praising life and hating mortality, the other wishing for the oblivion of death to come in an hour of crowning perfection; one which identifies the poet with the bird and its song, the other which

recognises their difference and separation. And three of the odes
started from a firm base in external reality. The nightingale had sung
in Hampstead the night before Keats began the poem: the ode to
Autumn was inspired by an autumnal landscape near Winchester:
the Grecian Urn almost certainly derived from memories of two
famous vases and a section of the Elgin marbles. It is not, of course,
that first-hand experience is necessary to trigger off a poem. The
point is that, when Keats started with such a concrete experience
rather than with an abstract idea, whether the experience was a
sight of Chapman's Homer or the sound of a real nightingale, the
resulting poem came superbly to life.

In the poem I have put at the end of this selection — a lyric
whose purity and simplicity may remind us of a song from a
Shakespeare play — occur the lines

> The feel of not to feel it,
> When there is none to heal it,
> Nor numbed sense to steel it,
> Was never said in rhyme.

Natural objects, the poem says, cannot remember past felicity.
Man remembers it all too well: and for him the worst thing is to
remember he was happy but not to be able to recall the 'feel' of that
happiness — to have the feeling of happiness replaced by a negative
but genuine sense of not being able to feel. This thought, in its
starkness and subtlety, gives us a pre-echo of modern poetry. It
reminds us, too, that truth to feeling was, above all, what Keats
aimed at and what in his best work he achieved.

To make a selection which shall be representative of a poet's
work is never easy. Should one, for instance, 'represent' the im-
mature or the inepter showings of a great writer? Clearly one could
not and would not wish to include the whole of *Endymion*; and I
think one can give the quality of 'Sleep and Poetry' and 'I Stood
Tip-toe', through extracts. I have put in 'Modern Love' and the
epistle to Reynolds, as sufficient examples of the way Keats' humour
and sense of fun, so sparkling in the prose letters, made heavier
going of verse. But what of the story poems or the two Hyperions?
Which would be more vandalistic — to offer them in truncated

form, or to omit one or two of them entirely? Well, I have compromised, being convinced that in any case the main object of a Selected Poems is to send the reader to the collected works.

C. Day Lewis

Lines from 'I Stood Tip-toe' (ll. 1–92)

I stood tip-toe upon a little hill,
The air was cooling, and so very still,
That the sweet buds which with a modest pride
Pull droopingly, in slanting curve aside,
Their scantly leaved, and finely tapering stems,
Had not yet lost those starry diadems
Caught from the early sobbing of the morn.
The clouds were pure and white as flocks new shorn,
And fresh from the clear brook; sweetly they slept
On the blue fields of heaven, and then there crept
A little noiseless noise among the leaves,
Born of the very sigh that silence heaves:
For not the faintest motion could be seen
Of all the shades that slanted o'er the green.
There was wide wand'ring for the greediest eye,
To peer about upon variety;
Far round the horizon's crystal air to skim,
And trace the dwindled edgings of its brim;
To picture out the quaint, and curious bending
Of a fresh woodland alley, never ending;
Or by the bowery clefts, and leafy shelves,
Guess where the jaunty streams refresh themselves.
I gazed awhile, and felt as light, and free
As though the fanning wings of Mercury
Had played upon my heels: I was light-hearted,
And many pleasures to my vision started;
So I straightway began to pluck a posey
Of luxuries bright, milky, soft and rosy.

A bush of May flowers with the bees about them;
Ah, sure no tasteful nook would be without them;
And let a lush laburnum oversweep them,
And let long grass grow round the roots to keep them
Moist, cool and green; and shade the violets,
That they may bind the moss in leafy nets.

A filbert hedge with wild briar overtwined,
And clumps of woodbine taking the soft wind
Upon their summer thrones; there too should be
The frequent chequer of a youngling tree,
That with a score of light green brethren shoots
From the quaint mossiness of aged roots:
Round which is heard a spring-head of clear waters
Babbling so wildly of its lovely daughters
The spreading blue bells: it may haply mourn
That such fair clusters should be rudely torn
From their fresh beds, and scattered thoughtlessly
By infant hands, left on the path to die.

Open afresh your round of starry folds,
Ye ardent marigolds!
Dry up the moisture from your golden lids,
For great Apollo bids
That in these days your praises should be sung
On many harps, which he has lately strung;
And when again your dewiness he kisses,
Tell him, I have you in my world of blisses:
So haply when I rove in some far vale,
His mighty voice may come upon the gale.

Here are sweet peas, on tip-toe for a flight:
With wings of gentle flush o'er delicate white,
And taper fingers catching at all things,
To bind them all about with tiny rings.

Linger awhile upon some bending planks
That lean against a streamlet's rushy banks,
And watch intently Nature's gentle doings:
They will be found softer than ring-dove's cooings.
How silent comes the water round that bend;
Not the minutest whisper does it send
To the o'erhanging sallows: blades of grass
Slowly across the chequer'd shadows pass.
Why, you might read two sonnets, ere they reach

To where the hurrying freshnesses aye preach
A natural sermon o'er their pebbly beds;
Where swarms of minnows show their little heads,
Staying their wavy bodies 'gainst the streams,
To taste the luxury of sunny beams
Temper'd with coolness. How they ever wrestle
With their own sweet delight, and ever nestle
Their silver bellies on the pebbly sand.
If you but scantily hold out the hand,
That very instant not one will remain;
But turn your eye, and they are there again.
The ripples seem right glad to reach those cresses,
And cool themselves among the em'rald tresses;
The while they cool themselves, they freshness give,
And moisture, that the bowery green may live:
So keeping up an interchange of favours,
Like good men in the truth of their behaviours.
Sometimes goldfinches one by one will drop
From low hung branches; little space they stop;
But sip, and twitter, and their feathers sleek;
Then off at once, as in a wanton freak:
Or perhaps, to show their black, and golden wings,
Pausing upon their yellow flutterings.

To G. A. W.

Nymph of the downward smile, and sidelong glance,
  In what diviner moments of the day
  Art thou most lovely? When gone far astray
Into the labyrinths of sweet utterance?
Or when serenely wand'ring in a trance
  Of sober thought? Or when starting away,
  With careless robe, to meet the morning ray,
Thou spar'st the flowers in thy mazy dance?
Haply 'tis when thy ruby lips part sweetly,

And so remain, because thou listenest:
But thou to please wert nurtured so completely
    That I can never tell what mood is best.
I shall as soon pronounce which Grace more neatly
    Trips it before Apollo than the rest.

'Keen, fitful gusts'

Keen, fitful gusts are whisp'ring here and there
    Among the bushes half leafless, and dry;
    The stars look very cold about the sky,
And I have many miles on foot to fare.
Yet feel I little of the cool bleak air,
    Or of the dead leaves rustling drearily,
    Or of those silver lamps that burn on high,
Or of the distance from home's pleasant lair:
For I am brimfull of the friendliness
    That in a little cottage I have found;
Of fair-hair'd Milton's eloquent distress,
    And all his love for gentle Lycid drown'd;
Of lovely Laura in her light green dress,
    And faithful Petrarch gloriously crown'd.

'To one who has been long'

To one who has been long in city pent,
    'Tis very sweet to look into the fair
    And open face of heaven, — to breathe a prayer
Full in the smile of the blue firmament.
Who is more happy, when, with heart's content,
    Fatigued he sinks into some pleasant lair
    Of wavy grass, and reads a debonair

And gentle tale of love and languishment?
Returning home at evening, with an ear
    Catching the notes of Philomel, — an eye
Watching the sailing cloudlet's bright career,
    He mourns that day so soon has glided by:
E'en like the passage of an angel's tear
    That falls through the clear ether silently.

On First Looking Into Chapman's Homer

Much have I travell'd in the realms of gold,
    And many goodly states and kingdoms seen;
    Round many western islands have I been
Which bards in fealty to Apollo hold.
Oft of one wide expanse had I been told
    That deep-brow'd Homer ruled as his demesne;
    Yet did I never breathe its pure serene
Till I heard Chapman speak out loud and bold:
Then felt I like some watcher of the skies
    When a new planet swims into his ken;
Or like stout Cortez when with eagle eyes
    He star'd at the Pacific — and all his men
Look'd at each other with a wild surmise —
    Silent, upon a peak in Darien.

On the Grasshopper and Cricket

The poetry of earth is never dead:
    When all the birds are faint with the hot sun,
    And hide in cooling trees, a voice will run
From hedge to hedge about the new-mown mead;

That is the Grasshopper's — he takes the lead
  In summer luxury, — he had never done
  With his delights; for when tired out with fun
He rests at ease beneath some pleasant weed.
The poetry of earth is ceasing never:
  On a lone winter evening, when the frost
    Has wrought a silence, from the stove there shrills
The Cricket's song, in warmth increasing ever,
    And seems to one in drowsiness half lost,
      The Grasshopper's among some grassy hills.

Lines from Sleep and Poetry (ll. 47–98)

O Poesy! for thee I hold my pen
That am not yet a glorious denizen
Of thy wide heaven — Should I rather kneel
Upon some mountain-top until I feel
A glowing splendour round about me hung,
And echo back the voice of thine own tongue?
O Poesy! for thee I grasp my pen
That am not yet a glorious denizen
Of thy wide heaven; yet, to my ardent prayer,
Yield from thy sanctuary some clear air,
Smoothed for intoxication by the breath
Of flowering bays, that I may die a death
Of luxury, and my young spirit follow
The morning sun-beams to the great Apollo
Like a fresh sacrifice; or, if I can bear
The o'erwhelming sweets, 'twill bring to me the fair
Visions of all places: a bowery nook
Will be elysium — an eternal book
Whence I may copy many a lovely saying
About the leaves, and flowers — about the playing
Of nymphs in woods, and fountains; and the shade

Keeping a silence round a sleeping maid;
And many a verse from so strange influence
That we must ever wonder how, and whence
It came. Also imaginings will hover
Round my fire-side, and haply there discover
Vistas of solemn beauty, where I'd wander
In happy silence, like the clear Meander
Through its lone vales; and where I found a spot
Of awfuller shade, or an enchanted grot,
Or a green hill o'erspread with chequered dress
Of flowers, and fearful from its loveliness,
Write on my tablets all that was permitted,
All that was for our human senses fitted.
Then the events of this wide world I'd seize
Like a strong giant, and my spirit teaze
Till at its shoulders it should proudly see
Wings to find out an immortality.

Stop and consider! life is but a day;
A fragile dew-drop on its perilous way
From a tree's summit; a poor Indian's sleep
While his boat hastens to the monstrous steep
Of Montmorenci. Why so sad a moan?
Life is the rose's hope while yet unblown;
The reading of an ever-changing tale;
The light uplifting of a maiden's veil;
A pigeon tumbling in clear summer air;
A laughing school-boy, without grief or care,
Riding the springy branches of an elm.

O for ten years, that I may overwhelm
Myself in poesy; so I may do the deed
That my own soul has to itself decreed.

Lines from Endymion, Book 1 (ll. 232–306)

'O thou, whose mighty palace roof doth hang
From jagged trunks, and overshadoweth
Eternal whispers, glooms, the birth, life, death
Of unseen flowers in heavy peacefulness;
Who lov'st to see the hamadryads dress
Their ruffled locks where meeting hazels darken;
And through whole solemn hours dost sit, and hearken
The dreary melody of bedded reeds —
In desolate places, where dank moisture breeds
The pipy hemlock to strange overgrowth;
Bethinking thee, how melancholy loth
Thou wast to lose fair Syrinx — do thou now,
By thy love's milky brow!
By all the trembling mazes that she ran,
Hear us, great Pan!

'O thou, for whose soul-soothing quiet, turtles
Passion their voices cooingly 'mong myrtles,
What time thou wanderest at eventide
Through sunny meadows, that outskirt the side
Of thine enmossed realms: O thou, to whom
Broad leaved fig trees even now foredoom
Their ripen'd fruitage; yellow girted bees
Their golden honeycombs; our village leas
Their fairest blossom'd beans and poppied corn;
The chuckling linnet its five young unborn,
To sing for thee; low creeping strawberries
Their summer coolness; pent up butterflies
Their freckled wings; yea, the fresh budding year
All its completions — be quickly near,
By every wind that nods the mountain pine,
O forester divine!

'Thou, to whom every faun and satyr flies
For willing service; whether to surprise

The squatted hare while in half sleeping fit;
Or upward ragged precipices flit
To save poor lambkins from the eagle's maw;
Or by mysterious enticement draw
Bewildered shepherds to their path again;
Or to tread breathless round the frothy main,
And gather up all fancifullest shells
For thee to tumble into Naiads' cells,
And, being hidden, laugh at their out-peeping;
Or to delight thee with fantastic leaping,
The while they pelt each other on the crown
With silvery oak apples, and fir cones brown —
By all the echoes that about thee ring,
Hear us, O satyr king!

  'O Hearkener to the loud clapping shears,
While ever and anon to his shorn peers
A ram goes bleating: Winder of the horn,
When snouted wild-boars routing tender corn
Anger our huntsmen: Breather round our farms,
To keep off mildews, and all weather harms:
Strange ministrant of undescribed sounds,
That come a swooning over hollow grounds,
And wither drearily on barren moors:
Dread opener of the mysterious doors
Leading to universal knowledge — see,
Great son of Dryope,
The many that are come to pay their vows
With leaves about their brows!

  'Be still the unimaginable lodge
For solitary thinkings; such as dodge
Conception to the very bourne of heaven,
Then leave the naked brain: be still the leaven,
That spreading in this dull and clodded earth
Gives it a touch ethereal — a new birth:
Be still a symbol of immensity;
A firmament reflected in a sea;

An element filling the space between;
An unknown — but no more: we humbly screen
With uplift hands our foreheads, lowly bending,
And giving out a shout most heaven rending,
Conjure thee to receive our humble Pæan,
Upon thy Mount Lycean!'

Lines from Endymion, Book 4 (ll. 146–290)

'O Sorrow,
    Why dost borrow
The natural hue of health, from vermeil lips? —
        To give maiden blushes
        To the white rose bushes?
Or is't thy dewy hand the daisy tips?

    'O Sorrow,
    Why dost borrow
The lustrous passion from a falcon-eye? —
        To give the glow-worm light?
        Or, on a moonless night,
To tinge, on syren shores, the salt sea-spry?

    'O Sorrow,
    Why dost borrow
The mellow ditties from a mourning tongue? —
        To give at evening pale
        Unto the nightingale,
That thou mayst listen the cold dews among?

    'O Sorrow,
    Why dost borrow
Heart's lightness from the merriment of May? —

A lover would not tread
A cowslip on the head,
Though he should dance from eve till peep of day —
Nor any drooping flower
Held sacred for thy bower,
Wherever he may sport himself and play.

'To Sorrow,
I bade good-morrow,
And thought to leave her far away behind;
But cheerly, cheerly,
She loves me dearly;
She is so constant to me, and so kind:
I would deceive her
And so leave her,
But ah! she is so constant and so kind.

'Beneath my palm trees, by the river side,
I sat a weeping: in the whole world wide
There was no one to ask me why I wept,—
And so I kept
Brimming the water-lily cups with tears
Cold as my fears.

'Beneath my palm trees, by the river side,
I sat aweeping: what enamour'd bride,
Cheated by shadowy wooer from the clouds,
But hides and shrouds
Beneath dark palm trees by a river side?

'And as I sat, over the light blue hills
There came a noise of revellers: the rills
Into the wide stream came of purple hue —
'Twas Bacchus and his crew!
The earnest trumpet spake, and silver thrills
From kissing cymbals made a merry din —
'Twas Bacchus and his kin!

Like to a moving vintage down they came,
Crown'd with green leaves, and faces all on flame;
All madly dancing through the pleasant valley,
    To scare thee, Melancholy!
O then, O then, thou wast a simple name!
And I forgot thee, as the berried holly
By shepherds is forgotten, when, in June,
Tall chestnuts keep away the sun and moon: —
    I rush'd into the folly!

'Within his car, aloft, young Bacchus stood,
Trifling his ivy-dart, in dancing mood,
    With sidelong laughing;
And little rills of crimson wine imbrued
His plump white arms, and shoulders, enough white
    For Venus' pearly bite:
And near him rode Silenus on his ass,
Pelted with flowers as he on did pass
    Tipsily quaffing.

'Whence came ye, merry Damsels! whence came ye!
So many, and so many, and such glee?
Why have ye left your bowers desolate,
    Your lutes, and gentler fate? —
"We follow Bacchus! Bacchus on the wing,
    A conquering!
Bacchus, young Bacchus! good or ill betide,
We dance before him thorough kingdoms wide: —
Come hither, lady fair, and joined be
    To our wild minstrelsy!"

'Whence came ye, jolly Satyrs! whence came ye!
So many, and so many, and such glee?
Why have ye left your forest haunts, why left
    Your nuts in oak-tree cleft? —

"For wine, for wine we left our kernel tree;
For wine we left our heath, and yellow brooms,
      And cold mushrooms;
For wine we follow Bacchus through the earth;
Great God of breathless cups and chirping mirth!—
Come hither, lady fair, and joined be
      To our mad minstrelsy!"

'Over wide streams and mountains great we went,
And, save when Bacchus kept his ivy tent,
Onward the tiger and the leopard pants,
      With Asian elephants:
Onward these myriads — with song and dance,
With zebras striped, and sleek Arabians' prance,
Web-footed alligators, crocodiles,
Bearing upon their scaly backs, in files,
Plump infant laughers mimicking the coil
Of seamen, and stout galley-rowers' toil:
With toying oars and silken sails they glide,
      Nor care for wind and tide.

'Mounted on panthers' furs and lions' manes,
From rear to van they scour about the plains;
A three days' journey in a moment done:
And always, at the rising of the sun,
About the wilds they hunt with spear and horn,
      On spleenful unicorn.

'I saw Osirian Egypt kneel adown
      Before the vine-wreath crown!
I saw parch'd Abyssinia rouse and sing
      To the silver cymbals' ring!
I saw the whelming vintage hotly pierce
      Old Tartary the fierce!
The kings of Inde their jewel-sceptres vail,
And from their treasures scatter pearled hail;
Great Brahma from his mystic heaven groans,
      And all his priesthood moans;

Before young Bacchus' eye-wink turning pale. —
Into these regions came I following him,
Sick hearted, weary — so I took a whim
To stray away into these forests drear
      Alone, without a peer:
And I have told thee all thou mayest hear.

      'Young stranger!
      I've been a ranger
In search of pleasure throughout every clime:
      Alas! 'tis not for me!
      Bewitch'd I sure must be,
To lose in grieving all my maiden prime.

      'Come then, Sorrow!
      Sweetest Sorrow!
Like an own babe I nurse thee on my breast:
      I thought to leave thee
      And deceive thee,
But now of all the world I love thee best.

      'There is not one,
      No, no, not one
But thee to comfort a poor lonely maid;
      Thou art her mother,
      And her brother,
Her playmate, and her wooer in the shade.'

On the Sea

It keeps eternal whisperings around
   Desolate shores, and with its mighty swell
   Gluts twice ten thousand caverns, till the spell
Of Hecate leaves them their old shadowy sound.
Often 'tis in such gentle temper found,
   That scarcely will the very smallest shell
   Be moved for days from where it sometime fell,
When last the winds of heaven were unbound.
Oh ye! who have your eye-balls vexed and tired,
   Feast them upon the wideness of the Sea;
     Oh ye! whose ears are dinn'd with uproar rude,
Or fed too much with cloying melody, —
     Sit ye near some old cavern's mouth, and brood
Until ye start, as if the sea-nymphs quired!

'When I have fears'

When I have fears that I may cease to be
   Before my pen has glean'd my teeming brain,
Before high-piled books, in charact'ry,
   Hold like rich garners the full-ripen'd grain;
When I behold, upon the night's starr'd face,
   Huge cloudy symbols of a high romance,
And think that I may never live to trace
   Their shadows, with the magic hand of chance;
And when I feel, fair creature of an hour!
   That I shall never look upon thee more,
Never have relish in the faery power
   Of unreflecting love! — then on the shore
Of the wide world I stand alone, and think
Till love and fame to nothingness do sink.

'The day is gone'

The day is gone, and all its sweets are gone!
  Sweet voice, sweet lips, soft hand, and softer breast,
Warm breath, light whisper, tender semi-tone,
  Bright eyes, accomplish'd shape, and lang'rous waist!
Faded the flower and all its budded charms,
  Faded the sight of beauty from my eyes,
Faded the shape of beauty from my arms,
  Faded the voice, warmth, whiteness, paradise —
Vanish'd unseasonably at shut of eve,
  When the dusk holiday — or holinight
Of fragrant-curtain'd love begins to weave
  The woof of darkness thick, for hid delight;
But, as I've read love's missal through to-day,
He'll let me sleep, seeing I fast and pray.

On Visiting the Tomb of Burns

The Town, the churchyard, and the setting sun,
  The clouds, the trees, the rounded hills all seem,
  Though beautiful, cold — strange — as in a dream,
I dreamed long ago, now new begun.
The short-liv'd, paly Summer is but won
  From Winter's ague, for one hour's gleam;
  Though sapphire-warm, their stars do never beam:
All is cold Beauty; pain is never done:
For who has mind to relish, Minos-wise,
  The real of Beauty, free from that dead hue
    Sickly imagination and sick pride
  Cast wan upon it? Burns! with honour due
    I oft have honour'd thee. Great shadow, hide
Thy face; I sin against thy native skies.

Old Meg

Old Meg she was a Gipsey,
  And liv'd upon the Moors;
Her bed it was the brown heath turf,
  And her house was out of doors.

Her apples were swart blackberries,
  Her currants, pods o' broom;
Her wine was dew of the wild white rose,
  Her book a churchyard tomb.

Her Brothers were the craggy hills,
  Her Sisters larchen trees;
Alone with her great family
  She liv'd as she did please.

No breakfast had she many a morn,
  No dinner many a noon,
And, 'stead of supper, she would stare
  Full hard against the Moon.

But every morn, of woodbine fresh
  She made her garlanding,
And, every night, the dark glen Yew
  She wove, and she would sing.

And with her fingers, old and brown,
  She plaited Mats o' Rushes,
And gave them to the Cottagers
  She met among the Bushes.

Old Meg was brave as Margaret Queen
  And tall as Amazon;
An old red blanket cloak she wore,
  A chip hat had she on.
God rest her aged bones somewhere!
  She died full long agone!

Modern Love

And what is love? It is a doll dress'd up
For idleness to cosset, nurse, and dandle;
A thing of soft misnomers, so divine
That silly youth doth think to make itself
Divine by loving, and so goes on
Yawning and doting a whole summer long,
Till Miss's comb is made a pearl tiara,
And common Wellingtons turn Romeo boots;
Till Cleopatra lives at number seven,
And Antony resides in Brunswick Square.
Fools! if some passions high have warm'd the world,
If Queens and Soldiers have play'd deep for hearts,
It is no reason why such agonies
Should be more common than the growth of weeds.
Fools! make me whole again that weighty pearl
The Queen of Egypt melted, and I'll say
That ye may love in spite of beaver hats.

To J. H. Reynolds, Esq.

Dear Reynolds, as last night I lay in bed,
There came before my eyes that wonted thread
Of Shapes, and Shadows and Remembrances,
That every other minute vex and please:
Things all disjointed come from North and south,
Two witch's eyes above a Cherub's mouth,
Voltaire with casque and shield and Habergeon,
And Alexander with his night-cap on —
Old Socrates a tying his cravat;
And Hazlitt playing with Miss Edgeworth's cat;
And Junius Brutus pretty well so, so,
Making the best of's way towards Soho.

Few are there who escape these visitings —
P'erhaps one or two, whose lives have patent wings;
And through whose curtains peeps no hellish nose,
No wild boar tushes, and no Mermaid's toes:
But flowers bursting out with lusty pride;
And young Æolian harps personified,
Some, Titian colours touch'd into real life. —
The sacrifice goes on; the pontiff knife
Gleams in the sun, the milk-white heifer lows,
The pipes go shrilly, the libation flows:
A white sail shews above the green-head cliff
Moves round the point, and throws her anchor stiff.
The Mariners join hymn with those on land. —
You know the Enchanted Castle it doth stand
Upon a Rock on the Border of a Lake
Nested in Trees, which all do seem to shake
From some old Magic like Urganda's sword.
O Phœbus that I had thy sacred word
To shew this Castle in fair dreaming wise
Unto my friend, while sick and ill he lies.
    You know it well enough, where it doth seem
A mossy place, a Merlin's Hall, a dream.
You know the clear Lake, and the little Isles,
The Mountains blue, and cold near neighbour rills —
All which elsewhere are but half animate
Here do they look alive to love and hate;
To smiles and frowns; they seem a lifted mound
Above some giant, pulsing underground.
    Part of the building was a chosen See
Built by a banish'd Santon of Chaldee:
The other part two thousand years from him
Was built by Cuthbert de Saint Aldebrim;
Then there's a little wing, far from the Sun,
Built by a Lapland Witch turn'd Maudlin nun —
And many other juts of aged stone
Founded with many a mason-devil's groan.
    The doors all look as if they oped themselves,
The windows as if latch'd by fays & elves —

And from them comes a silver flash of light
As from the Westward of a Summer's night;
Or like a beauteous woman's large blue eyes
Gone mad through olden songs and Poesies —
    See what is coming from the distance dim!
A golden galley all in silken trim!
Three rows of oars are lightening moment-whiles
Into the verdurous bosoms of those Isles.
Towards the Shade under the Castle Wall
It comes in silence — now tis hidden all.
The clarion sounds; and from a postern grate
An echo of sweet music doth create
A fear in the poor herdsman who doth bring
His beasts to trouble the enchanted spring:
He tells of the sweet music and the spot
To all his friends, and they believe him not.
    O that our dreamings all of sleep or wake
Would all their colours from the Sunset take:
From something of material sublime,
Rather than shadow our own Soul's daytime
In the dark void of Night. For in the world
We jostle — but my flag is not unfurl'd
On the Admiral staff — and to philosophize
I dare not yet! — Oh never will the prize,
High reason, and the lore of good and ill
Be my award. Things cannot to the will
Be settled, but they tease us out of thought.
Or is it that Imagination brought
Beyond its proper bound, yet still confined, —
Lost in a sort of Purgatory blind,
Cannot refer to any standard law
Of either earth or heaven? — It is a flaw
In happiness to see beyond our bourn —
It forces us in Summer skies to mourn:
It spoils the singing of the Nightingale.
    Dear Reynolds, I have a mysterious tale
And cannot speak it. The first page I read
Upon a Lampit Rock of green sea weed

Among the breakers — 'Twas a quiet Eve;
The rocks were silent — the wide sea did weave
An untumultuous fringe of silver foam
Along the flat brown sand. I was at home,
And should have been most happy — but I saw
Too far into the sea; where every maw
The greater on the less feeds evermore:—
But I saw too distinct into the core
Of an eternal fierce destruction,
And so from Happiness I far was gone.
Still am I sick of it: and though to-day
I've gathered young spring-leaves, and flowers gay
Of Periwinkle and wild strawberry,
Still do I that most fierce destruction see,
The Shark at savage prey — the hawk at pounce,
The gentle Robin, like a pard or ounce,
Ravening a worm — Away ye horrid moods,
Moods of one's mind! You know I hate them well,
You know I'd sooner be a clapping bell
To some Kamschatkan missionary church,
Than with these horrid moods be left in lurch —
Do you get health — and Tom the same — I'll dance,
And from detested moods in new Romance
Take refuge — Of bad lines a Centaine dose
Is sure enough — and so 'here follows prose'. —

Lamia

PART I

Upon a time, before the faery broods
Drove Nymph and Satyr from the prosperous woods,
Before King Oberon's bright diadem,
Sceptre, and mantle, clasp'd with dewy gem,
Frighted away the Dryads and the Fauns
From rushes green, and brakes, and cowslip'd lawns,
The ever-smitten Hermes empty left
His golden throne, bent warm on amorous theft:
From high Olympus had he stolen light,
On this side of Jove's clouds, to escape the sight
Of his great summoner, and made retreat
Into a forest on the shores of Crete.
For somewhere in that sacred island dwelt
A nymph, to whom all hoofed Satyrs knelt;
At whose white feet the languid Tritons poured
Pearls, while on land they wither'd and adored.
Fast by the springs where she to bathe was wont,
And in those meads where sometime she might haunt,
Were strewn rich gifts, unknown to any Muse,
Though Fancy's casket were unlock'd to choose.
Ah, what a world of love was at her feet!
So Hermes thought, and a celestial heat
Burnt from his winged heels to either ear,
That from a whiteness, as the lily clear,
Blush'd into roses 'mid his golden hair,
Fallen in jealous curls about his shoulders bare.
From vale to vale, from wood to wood, he flew,
Breathing upon the flowers his passion new,
And wound with many a river to its head,
To find where this sweet nymph prepar'd her secret bed:
In vain; the sweet nymph might nowhere be found,
And so he rested, on the lonely ground,
Pensive, and full of painful jealousies

Of the Wood-Gods, and even the very trees.
There as he stood, he heard a mournful voice,
Such as once heard, in gentle heart, destroys
All pain but pity: thus the lone voice spake:
'When from this wreathed tomb shall I awake!
'When move in a sweet body fit for life,
'And love, and pleasure, and the ruddy strife
'Of hearts and lips! Ah, miserable me!'
The God, dove-footed, glided silently
Round bush and tree, soft-brushing, in his speed,
The taller grasses and full-flowering weed,
Until he found a palpitating snake,
Bright, and cirque-couchant in a dusky brake.

She was a gordian shape of dazzling hue,
Vermilion-spotted, golden, green, and blue;
Striped like a zebra, freckled like a pard,
Eyed like a peacock, and all crimson barr'd;
And full of silver moons, that, as she breathed,
Dissolv'd, or brighter shone, or interwreathed
Their lustres with the gloomier tapestries —
So rainbow-sided, touch'd with miseries,
She seem'd, at once, some penanced lady elf,
Some demon's mistress, or the demon's self.
Upon her crest she wore a wannish fire
Sprinkled with stars, like Ariadne's tiar:
Her head was serpent, but ah, bitter-sweet!
She had a woman's mouth with all its pearls complete:
And for her eyes: what could such eyes do there
But weep, and weep, that they were born so fair?
As Proserpine still weeps for her Sicilian air.
Her throat was serpent, but the words she spake
Came, as through bubbling honey, for Love's sake,
And thus; while Hermes on his pinions lay,
Like a stoop'd falcon ere he takes his prey.

'Fair Hermes, crown'd with feathers, fluttering light,
'I had a splendid dream of thee last night:

'I saw thee sitting, on a throne of gold,
'Among the Gods, upon Olympus old,
'The only sad one; for thou didst not hear
'The soft, lute-finger'd Muses chaunting clear,
'Nor even Apollo when he sang alone,
'Deaf to his throbbing throat's long, long melodious moan.
'I dreamt I saw thee, robed in purple flakes,
'Break amorous through the clouds, as morning breaks,
'And, swiftly as a bright Phœbean dart,
'Strike for the Cretan isle; and here thou art!
'Too gentle Hermes, hast thou found the maid?'
Whereat the star of Lethe not delay'd
His rosy eloquence, and thus inquired:
'Thou smooth-lipp'd serpent, surely high inspired!
'Thou beauteous wreath, with melancholy eyes,
'Possess whatever bliss thou canst devise,
'Telling me only where my nymph is fled, —
'Where she doth breathe!' 'Bright planet, thou hast said,'
Return'd the snake, 'but seal with oaths, fair God!'
'I swear,' said Hermes, 'by my serpent rod,
'And by thine eyes, and by thy starry crown!'
Light flew his earnest words, among the blossoms blown.
Then thus again the brilliance feminine:
'Too frail of heart! for this lost nymph of thine,
'Free as the air, invisibly, she strays
'About these thornless wilds; her pleasant days
'She tastes unseen; unseen her nimble feet
'Leave traces in the grass and flowers sweet;
'From weary tendrils, and bow'd branches green,
'She plucks the fruit unseen, she bathes unseen:
'And by my power is her beauty veil'd
'To keep it unaffronted, unassail'd
'By the love-glances of unlovely eyes,
'Of Satyrs, Fauns, and blear'd Silenus' sighs.
'Pale grew her immortality, for woe
'Of all these lovers, and she grieved so
'I took compassion on her, bade her steep
'Her hair in weïrd syrops, that would keep

'Her loveliness invisible, yet free
'To wander as she loves, in liberty.
'Thou shalt behold her, Hermes, thou alone,
'If thou wilt, as thou swearest, grant my boon!'
Then, once again, the charmed God began
An oath, and through the serpent's ears it ran
Warm, tremulous, devout, psalterian.
Ravish'd, she lifted her Circean head,
Blush'd a live damask, and swift-lisping said,
'I was a woman, let me have once more
'A woman's shape, and charming as before.
'I love a youth of Corinth — O the bliss!
'Give me my woman's form, and place me where he is.
'Stoop, Hermes, let me breathe upon thy brow,
'And thou shalt see thy sweet nymph even now.'
The God on half-shut feathers sank serene,
She breath'd upon his eyes, and swift was seen
Of both the guarded nymph near-smiling on the green.
It was no dream; or say a dream it was,
Real are the dreams of Gods, and smoothly pass
Their pleasures in a long immortal dream.
One warm, flush'd moment, hovering, it might seem
Dash'd by the wood-nymph's beauty, so he burn'd;
Then, lighting on the printless verdure, turn'd
To the swoon'd serpent, and with languid arm,
Delicate, put to proof the lythe Caducean charm.
So done, upon the nymph his eyes he bent
Full of adoring tears and blandishment,
And towards her stept: she, like a moon in wane,
Faded before him, cower'd, nor could restrain
Her fearful sobs, self-folding like a flower
That faints into itself at evening hour:
But the God fostering her chilled hand;
She felt the warmth, her eyelids open'd bland,
And, like new flowers at morning song of bees,
Bloom'd, and gave up her honey to the lees.
Into the green-recessed woods they flew;
Nor grew they pale, as mortal lovers do.

Left to herself, the serpent now began
To change; her elfin blood in madness ran,
Her mouth foam'd, and the grass, therewith besprent,
Wither'd at dew so sweet and virulent;
Her eyes in torture fix'd, and anguish drear,
Hot, glaz'd, and wide, with lid-lashes all sear,
Flash'd phosphor and sharp sparks, without one cooling tear.
The colours all inflam'd throughout her train,
She writh'd about, convuls'd with scarlet pain:
A deep volcanian yellow took the place
Of all her milder-mooned body's grace;
And, as the lava ravishes the mead,
Spoilt all her silver mail, and golden brede,
Made gloom of all her frecklings, streaks and bars,
Eclips'd her crescents, and lick'd up her stars:
So that, in moments few, she was undrest
Of all her sapphires, greens, and amethyst,
And rubious-argent: of all these bereft,
Nothing but pain and ugliness were left.
Still shone her crown; that vanish'd, also she
Melted and disappear'd as suddenly;
And in the air, her new voice luting soft,
Cried, 'Lycius! gentle Lycius!' — Borne aloft
With the bright mists about the mountains hoar
These words dissolv'd: Crete's forests heard no more.

Whither fled Lamia, now a lady bright,
A full-born beauty new and exquisite?
She fled into that valley they pass o'er
Who go to Corinth from Cenchreas' shore;
And rested at the foot of those wild hills,
The rugged founts of the Peræan rills,
And of that other ridge whose barren back
Stretches, with all its mist and cloudy rack,
South-westward to Cleone. There she stood
About a young bird's flutter from a wood,
Fair, on a sloping green of mossy tread,
By a clear pool, wherein she passioned

To see herself escap'd from so sore ills,
While her robes flaunted with the daffodils.

Ah, happy Lycius! — for she was a maid
More beautiful than ever twisted braid,
Or sigh'd, or blush'd, or on spring-flowered lea
Spread a green kirtle to the minstrelsy:
A virgin purest lipp'd, yet in the lore
Of love deep learned to the red heart's core:
Not one hour old, yet of sciential brain
To unperplex bliss from its neighbour pain;
Define their pettish limits, and estrange
Their points of contact, and swift counterchange;
Intrigue with the specious chaos, and dispart
Its most ambiguous atoms with sure art;
As though in Cupid's college she had spent
Sweet days a lovely graduate, still unshent,
And kept his rosy terms in idle languishment.

Why this fair creature chose so fairily
By the wayside to linger, we shall see;
But first 'tis fit to tell how she could muse
And dream, when in the serpent prison-house,
Of all she list, strange or magnificent:
How, ever, where she will'd, her spirit went;
Whether to faint Elysium, or where
Down through tress-lifting waves the Nereids fair
Wind into Thetis' bower by many a pearly stair;
Or where God Bacchus drains his cups divine,
Stretch'd out, at ease, beneath a glutinous pine;
Or where in Pluto's gardens palatine
Mulciber's columns gleam in far piazzian line.
And sometimes into cities she would send
Her dream, with feast and rioting to blend;
And once, while among mortals dreaming thus,
She saw the young Corinthian Lycius
Charioting foremost in the envious race,
Like a young Jove with calm uneager face,

And fell into a swooning love of him.
Now on the moth-time of that evening dim
He would return that way, as well she knew,
To Corinth from the shore; for freshly blew
 The eastern soft wind, and his galley now
Grated the quaystones with her brazen prow
In port Cenchreas, from Egina isle
Fresh anchor'd; whither he had been awhile
To sacrifice to Jove, whose temple there
Waits with high marble doors for blood and incense rare.
Jove heard his vows, and better'd his desire;
For by some freakful chance he made retire
From his companions, and set forth to walk,
Perhaps grown wearied of their Corinth talk:
Over the solitary hills he fared,
Thoughtless at first, but ere eve's star appeared
His phantasy was lost, where reason fades,
In the calm'd twilight of Platonic shades.
Lamia beheld him coming, near, more near —
Close to her passing, in indifference drear,
His silent sandals swept the mossy green;
So neighbour'd to him, and yet so unseen
She stood: he pass'd, shut up in mysteries,
His mind wrapp'd like his mantle, while her eyes
Follow'd his steps, and her neck regal white
Turn'd — syllabling thus, 'Ah, Lycius bright,
'And will you leave me on the hills alone?
'Lycius, look back! and be some pity shown.'
He did; not with cold wonder fearingly,
But Orpheus-like at an Eurydice;
For so delicious were the words she sung,
It seem'd he had lov'd them a whole summer long:
And soon his eyes had drunk her beauty up,
Leaving no drop in the bewildering cup,
And still the cup was full, — while he, afraid
Lest she should vanish ere his lip had paid
Due adoration, thus began to adore;
Her soft look growing coy, she saw his chain so sure:

'Leave thee alone! Look back! Ah, Goddess, see
'Whether my eyes can ever turn from thee!
'For pity do not this sad heart belie —
'Even as thou vanishest so I shall die.
'Stay! though a Naiad of the rivers, stay!
'To thy far wishes will thy streams obey:
'Stay! though the greenest woods be thy domain,
'Alone they can drink up the morning rain:
'Though a descended Pleiad, will not one
'Of thine harmonious sisters keep in tune
'Thy spheres, and as thy silver proxy shine?
'So sweetly to these ravish'd ears of mine
'Came thy sweet greeting, that if thou shouldst fade
'Thy memory will waste me to a shade: —
'For pity do not melt!' — 'If I should stay,'
Said Lamia, 'here, upon this floor of clay,
'And pain my steps upon these flowers too rough,
'What canst thou say or do of charm enough
'To dull the nice remembrance of my home?
'Thou canst not ask me with thee here to roam
'Over these hills and vales, where no joy is, —
'Empty of immortality and bliss!
'Thou art a scholar, Lycius, and must know
'That finer spirits cannot breathe below
'In human climes, and live: Alas! poor youth,
'What taste of purer air hast thou to soothe
'My essence? What serener palaces,
'Where I may all my many senses please,
'And by mysterious sleights a hundred thirsts appease?
'It cannot be — Adieu!' So said, she rose
Tiptoe with white arms spread. He, sick to lose
The amorous promise of her lone complain,
Swoon'd, murmuring of love, and pale with pain.
The cruel lady, without any show
Of sorrow for her tender favourite's woe,
But rather, if her eyes could brighter be,
With brighter eyes and slow amenity,
Put her new lips to his, and gave afresh

The life she had so tangled in her mesh:
And as he from one trance was wakening
Into another, she began to sing,
Happy in beauty, life, and love, and every thing,
A song of love, too sweet for earthly lyres,
While, like held breath, the stars drew in their panting fires.
And then she whisper'd in such trembling tone,
As those who, safe together met alone
For the first time through many anguish'd days,
Use other speech than looks; bidding him raise
His drooping head, and clear his soul of doubt,
For that she was a woman, and without
Any more subtle fluid in her veins
Than throbbing blood, and that the self-same pains
Inhabited her frail-strung heart as his.
And next she wonder'd how his eyes could miss
Her face so long in Corinth, where, she said,
She dwelt but half retir'd, and there had led
Days happy as the gold coin could invent
Without the aid of love; yet in content
Till she saw him, as once she pass'd him by,
Where 'gainst a column he leant thoughtfully
At Venus' temple porch, 'mid baskets heap'd
Of amorous herbs and flowers, newly reap'd
Late on that eve, as 'twas the night before
The Adonian feast; whereof she saw no more,
But wept alone those days, for why should she adore?
Lycius from death awoke into amaze,
To see her still, and singing so sweet lays;
Then from amaze into delight he fell
To hear her whisper woman's lore so well;
And every word she spake entic'd him on
To unperplex'd delight and pleasure known.
Let the mad poets say whate'er they please
Of the sweets of Fairies, Peris, Goddesses,
There is not such a treat among them all,
Haunters of cavern, lake, and waterfall,
As a real woman, lineal indeed

From Pyrrha's pebbles or old Adam's seed.
Thus gentle Lamia judg'd, and judg'd aright,
That Lycius could not love in half a fright,
So threw the goddess off, and won his heart
More pleasantly by playing woman's part,
With no more awe than what her beauty gave,
That, while it smote, still guaranteed to save.
Lycius to all made eloquent reply,
Marrying to every word a twinborn sigh;
And last, pointing to Corinth, ask'd her sweet,
If 'twas too far that night for her soft feet.
The way was short, for Lamias's eagerness
Made, by a spell, the triple league decrease
To a few paces; not at all surmised
By blinded Lycius, so in her comprized.
They pass'd the city gates, he knew not how,
So noiseless, and he never thought to know.

As men talk in a dream, so Corinth all,
Throughout her palaces imperial,
And all her populous streets and temples lewd,
Mutter'd, like tempest in the distance brew'd,
To the wide-spreaded night above her towers.
Men, women, rich and poor, in the cool hours,
Shuffled their sandals o'er the pavement white,
Companion'd or alone; while many a light
Flared, here and there, from wealthy festivals,
And threw their moving shadows on the walls,
Or found them cluster'd in the corniced shade
Of some arch'd temple door, or dusky colonnade.

Muffling his face, of greeting friends in fear,
Her fingers he press'd hard, as one came near
With curl'd gray beard, sharp eyes, and smooth bald crown,
Slow-stepp'd, and robed in philosophic gown:
Lycius shrank closer, as they met and past,
Into his mantle, adding wings to haste,
While hurried Lamia trembled: 'Ah,' said he,

'Why do you shudder, love, so ruefully?
'Why does your tender palm dissolve in dew?' —
'I'm wearied,' said fair Lamia: 'tell me who
'Is that old man? I cannot bring to mind
'His features: — Lycius! wherefore did you blind
'Yourself from his quick eyes?' Lycius replied,
''Tis Apollonius sage, my trusty guide
'And good instructor; but to-night he seems
'The ghost of folly haunting my sweet dreams.'

  While yet he spake they had arrived before
A pillar'd porch, with lofty portal door,
Where hung a silver lamp, whose phosphor glow
Reflected in the slabbed steps below,
Mild as a star in water; for so new,
And so unsullied was the marble hue,
So through the crystal polish, liquid fine,
Ran the dark veins, that none but feet divine
Could e'er have touch'd there. Sounds Æolian
Breath'd from the hinges, as the ample span
Of the wide doors disclos'd a place unknown
Some time to any, but those two alone,
And a few Persian mutes, who that same year
Were seen about the markets: none knew where
They could inhabit; the most curious
Were foil'd, who watch'd to trace them to their house:
And but the flitter-winged verse must tell
For truth's sake, what woe afterwards befel,
'Twould humour many a heart to leave them thus,
Shut from the busy world of more incredulous.

PART II

Love in a hut, with water and a crust,
Is — Love, forgive us! — cinders, ashes, dust;
Love in a palace is perhaps at last
More grievous torment than a hermit's fast: —
That is a doubtful tale from faery land,

48

Hard for the non-elect to understand.
Had Lycius liv'd to hand his story down,
He might have given the moral a fresh frown,
Or clench'd it quite: but too short was their bliss
To breed distrust and hate, that make the soft voice hiss.
Besides, there, nightly, with terrific glare,
Love, jealous grown of so complete a pair,
Hover'd and buzz'd his wings, with fearful roar,
Above the lintel of their chamber door,
And down the passage cast a glow upon the floor.

    For all this came a ruin: side by side
They were enthroned, in the even tide,
Upon a couch, near to a curtaining
Whose airy texture, from a golden string,
Floated into the room, and let appear
Unveil'd the summer heaven, blue and clear,
Betwixt two marble shafts: — there they reposed,
Where use had made it sweet, with eyelids closed,
Saving a tythe which love still open kept,
That they might see each other while they almost slept;
When from the slope side of a suburb hill,
Deafening the swallow's twitter, came a thrill
Of trumpets — Lycius started — the sounds fled,
But left a thought a-buzzing in his head.
For the first time, since first he harbour'd in
That purple-lined palace of sweet sin,
His spirit pass'd beyond its golden bourn
Into the noisy world almost forsworn.
The lady, ever watchful, penetrant,
Saw this with pain, so arguing a want
Of something more, more than her empery
Of joys; and she began to moan and sigh
Because he mused beyond her, knowing well
That but a moment's thought is passion's passing bell.
'Why do you sigh, fair creature?' whisper'd he:
'Why do you think?' return'd she tenderly:
'You have deserted me; — where am I now?

'Not in your heart while care weighs on your brow:
'No, no, you have dismiss'd me; and I go
'From your breast houseless: ay, it must be so.'
He answer'd, bending to her open eyes,
Where he was mirror'd small in paradise,
'My silver planet, both of eve and morn!
'Why will you plead yourself so sad forlorn,
'While I am striving how to fill my heart
'With deeper crimson, and a double smart?
'How to entangle, trammel up and snare
'Your soul in mine, and labyrinth you there
'Like the hid scent in an unbudded rose?
'Ay, a sweet kiss — you see your mighty woes.
'My thoughts! shall I unveil them? Listen then!
'What mortal hath a prize, that other men
'May be confounded and abash'd withal,
'But lets it sometimes pace abroad majestical,
'And triumph, as in thee I should rejoice
'Amid the hoarse alarm of Corinth's voice.
'Let my foes choke, and my friends shout afar,
'While through the thronged streets your bridal car
'Wheels round its dazzling spokes.' — The lady's cheek
Trembled; she nothing said, but, pale and meek,
Arose and knelt before him, wept a rain
Of sorrows at his words; at last with pain
Beseeching him, the while his hand she wrung,
To change his purpose. He thereat was stung,
Perverse, with stronger fancy to reclaim
Her wild and timid nature to his aim:
Besides, for all his love, in self despite
Against his better self, he took delight
Luxurious in her sorrows, soft and new.
His passion, cruel grown, took on a hue
Fierce and sanguineous as 'twas possible
In one whose brow had no dark veins to swell.
Fine was the mitigated fury, like
Apollo's presence when in act to strike
The serpent — Ha, the serpent! certes, she

Was none. She burnt, she lov'd the tyranny,
And, all subdued, consented to the hour
When to the bridal he should lead his paramour.
Whispering in midnight silence, said the youth,
'Sure some sweet name thou hast, though, by my truth,
'I have not ask'd it, ever thinking thee
'Not mortal, but of heavenly progeny,
'As still I do. Hast any mortal name,
'Fit appellation for this dazzling frame?
'Or friends or kinsfolk on the citied earth,
'To share our marriage feast and nuptial mirth?'
'I have no friends,' said Lamia, 'no, not one;
'My presence in wide Corinth hardly known:
'My parents' bones are in their dusty urns
'Sepulchred, where no kindled incense burns,
'Seeing all their luckless race are dead, save me,
'And I neglect the holy rite for thee.
'Even as you list invite your many guests;
'But if, as now it seems, your vision rests
'With any pleasure on me, do not bid
'Old Apollonius — from him keep me hid.'
Lycius, perplex'd at words so blind and blank,
Made close inquiry; from whose touch she shrank,
Feigning a sleep; and he to the dull shade
Of deep sleep in a moment was betray'd.

　　It was the custom then to bring away
The bride from home at blushing shut of day,
Veil'd, in a chariot, heralded along
By strewn flowers, torches, and a marriage song,
With other pageants: but this fair unknown
Had not a friend. So being left alone,
(Lycius was gone to summon all his kin)
And knowing surely she could never win
His foolish heart from its mad pompousness,
She set herself, high-thoughted, how to dress
The misery in fit magnificence.
She did so, but 'tis doubtful how and whence

Came, and who were her subtle servitors.
About the halls, and to and from the doors,
There was a noise of wings, till in short space
The glowing banquet-room shone with wide-arched grace.
A haunting music, sole perhaps and lone
Supportress of the faery-roof, made moan
Throughout, as fearful the whole charm might fade.
Fresh carved cedar, mimicking a glade
Of palm and plantain, met from either side,
High in the midst, in honour of the bride:
Two palms and then two plantains, and so on,
From either side their stems branch'd one to one
All down the aisled place; and beneath all
There ran a stream of lamps straight on from wall to wall.
So canopied, lay an untasted feast
Teeming with odours. Lamia, regal drest,
Silently paced about, and as she went,
In pale contented sort of discontent,
Mission'd her viewless servants to enrich
The fretted splendour of each nook and niche.
Between the tree-stems, marbled plain at first,
Came jasper pannels; then, anon, there burst
Forth creeping imagery of slighter trees,
And with the larger wove in small intricacies.
Approving all, she faded at self-will,
And shut the chamber up, close, hush'd and still.
Complete and ready for the revels rude,
When dreadful guests would come to spoil her solitude.

    The day appear'd, and all the gossip rout.
O senseless Lycius! Madman! wherefore flout
The silent-blessing fate, warm cloister'd hours,
And show to common eyes these secret bowers?
The herd approach'd; each guest, with busy brain,
Arriving at the portal, gaz'd amain,
And enter'd marveling: for they knew the street,
Remember'd it from childhood all complete
Without a gap, yet ne'er before had seen

That royal porch, that high-built fair demesne;
So in they hurried all, maz'd, curious and keen:
Save one, who look'd thereon with eye severe,
And with calm-planted steps walk'd in austere;
'Twas Apollonius: something too he laugh'd,
As though some knotty problem, that had daft
His patient thought, had now begun to thaw,
And solve and melt: — 'twas just as he foresaw.

He met within the murmurous vestibule
His young disciple. "Tis no common rule,
'Lycius,' said he, 'for uninvited guest
'To force himself upon you, and infest
'With an unbidden presence the bright throng
'Of younger friends; yet must I do this wrong,
'And you forgive me.' Lycius blush'd, and led
The old man through the inner doors broad-spread;
With reconciling words and courteous mien
Turning into sweet milk the sophist's spleen.

Of wealthy lustre was the banquet-room,
Fill'd with pervading brilliance and perfume:
Before each lucid pannel fuming stood
A censer fed with myrrh and spiced wood,
Each by a sacred tripod held aloft,
Whose slender feet wide-swerv'd upon the soft
Wool-woofed carpets: fifty wreaths of smoke
From fifty censers their light voyage took
To the high roof, still mimick'd as they rose
Along the mirror'd walls by twin-clouds odorous.
Twelve sphered tables, by silk seats insphered,
High as the level of a man's breast rear'd
On libbard's paws, upheld the heavy gold
Of cups and goblets, and the store thrice told
Of Ceres' horn, and, in huge vessels, wine
Come from the gloomy tun with merry shine.
Thus loaded with a feast the tables stood,
Each shrining in the midst the image of a God

When in an antichamber every guest
Had felt the cold full sponge to pleasure press'd,
By minist'ring slaves, upon his hands and feet,
And fragrant oils with ceremony meet
Pour'd on his hair, they all mov'd to the feast
In white robes, and themselves in order placed
Around the silken couches, wondering
Whence all this mighty cost and blaze of wealth could spring.

Soft went the music the soft air along,
While fluent Greek a vowel'd undersong
Kept up among the guests, discoursing low
At first, for scarcely was the wine at flow;
But when the happy vintage touch'd their brains,
Louder they talk, and louder come the strains
Of powerful instruments: — the gorgeous dyes,
The space, the splendour of the draperies,
The roof of awful richness, nectarous cheer,
Beautiful slaves, and Lamia's self, appear,
Now, when the wine has done its rosy deed,
And every soul from human trammels freed,
No more so strange; for merry wine, sweet wine,
Will make Elysian shades not too fair, too divine.
Soon was God Bacchus at meridian height;
Flush'd were their cheeks, and bright eyes double bright:
Garlands of every green, and every scent
From vales deflower'd, or forest-trees branch-rent,
In baskets of bright osier'd gold were brought
High as the handles heap'd, to suit the thought
Of every guest; that each, as he did please,
Might fancy-fit his brows, silk-pillow'd at his ease.

What wreath for Lamia? What for Lycius?
What for the sage, old Apollonius?
Upon her aching forehead be there hung
The leaves of willow and of adder's tongue;
And for the youth, quick, let us strip for him
The thyrsus, that his watching eyes may swim

Into forgetfulness; and, for the sage,
Let spear-grass and the spiteful thistle wage
War on his temples. Do not all charms fly
At the mere touch of cold philosophy?
There was an awful rainbow once in heaven:
We know her woof, her texture; she is given
In the dull catalogue of common things.
Philosophy will clip an Angel's wings,
Conquer all mysteries by rule and line,
Empty the haunted air, and gnomed mine —
Unweave a rainbow, as it erewhile made
The tender-person'd Lamia melt into a shade.

By her glad Lycius sitting, in chief place,
Scarce saw in all the room another face,
Till, checking his love trance, a cup he took
Full brimm'd, and opposite sent forth a look
'Cross the broad table, to beseech a glance
From his old teacher's wrinkled countenance,
And pledge him. The bald-head philosopher
Had fix'd his eye, without a twinkle or stir
Full on the alarmed beauty of the bride,
Brow-beating her fair form, and troubling her sweet pride.
Lycius then press'd her hand, with devout touch,
As pale it lay upon the rosy couch:
'Twas icy, and the cold ran through his veins;
Then sudden it grew hot, and all the pains
Of an unnatural heat shot to his heart.
'Lamia, what means this? Wherefore dost thou start?
'Know'st thou that man?' Poor Lamia answer'd not.
He gaz'd into her eyes, and not a jot
Own'd they the lovelorn piteous appeal:
More, more he gaz'd: his human senses reel:
Some hungry spell that loveliness absorbs;
There was no recognition in those orbs.
'Lamia!' he cried — and no soft-toned reply.
The many heard, and the loud revelry
Grew hush; the stately music no more breathes;

The myrtle sicken'd in a thousand wreaths.
By faint degrees, voice, lute, and pleasure ceased;
A deadly silence step by step increased,
Until it seem'd a horrid presence there,
And not a man but felt the terror in his hair.
'Lamia!' he shriek'd; and nothing but the shriek
With its sad echo did the silence break.
'Begone, foul dream!' he cried, gazing again
In the bride's face, where now no azure vein
Wander'd on fair-spaced temples; no soft bloom
Misted the cheek; no passion to illume
The deep-recessed vision: — all was blight;
Lamia, no longer fair, there sat a deadly white.
'Shut, shut those juggling eyes, thou ruthless man!
'Turn them aside, wretch! or the righteous ban
'Of all the Gods, whose dreadful images
'Here represent their shadowy presences,
'May pierce them on the sudden with the thorn
'Of painful blindness; leaving thee forlorn,
'In trembling dotage to the feeblest fright
'Of conscience, for their long offended might,
'For all thine impious proud-heart sophistries,
'Unlawful magic, and enticing lies.
'Corinthians! look upon that gray-beard wretch!
'Mark how, possess'd, his lashless eyelids stretch
'Around his demon eyes! Corinthians, see!
'My sweet bride withers at their potency.'
'Fool!' said the sophist, in an under-tone
Gruff with contempt; which a death-nighing moan
From Lycius answer'd, as heart-struck and lost,
He sank supine beside the aching ghost.
'Fool! Fool!' repeated he, while his eyes still
Relented not, nor mov'd; 'from every ill
'Of life have I preserv'd thee to this day,
'And shall I see thee made a serpent's prey?'
Then Lamia breath'd death breath; the sophist's eye,
Like a sharp spear, went through her utterly,
Keen, cruel, perceant, stinging: she, as well

As her weak hand could any meaning tell,
Motion'd him to be silent; vainly so,
He look'd and look'd again a level — No!
'A Serpent!' echoed he; no sooner said,
Than with a frightful scream she vanished:
And Lycius' arms were empty of delight,
As were his limbs of life, from that same night.
On the high couch he lay! — his friends came round —
Supported him — no pulse, or breath they found,
And, in its marriage robe, the heavy body wound.

Lines from Isabella (stanzas 26–30 and 43–53)

XXVI

'Love, Isabel!' said he, 'I was in pain
  'Lest I should miss to bid thee a good morrow
'Ah! what if I should lose thee, when so fain
  'I am to stifle all the heavy sorrow
'Of a poor three hours' absence? but we'll gain
  'Out of the amorous dark what day doth borrow.
'Good bye! I'll soon be back.' — 'Good bye!' said she: —
And as he went she chanted merrily.

XXVII

So the two brothers and their murder'd man
  Rode past fair Florence, to where Arno's stream
Gurgles through straiten'd banks, and still doth fan
  Itself with dancing bulrush, and the bream
Keeps head against the freshets. Sick and wan
  The brothers' faces in the ford did seem,
Lorenzo's flush with love. — They pass'd the water
Into a forest quiet for the slaughter.

XXVIII

There was Lorenzo slain and buried in,
　　There in that forest did his great love cease;
Ah! when a soul doth thus its freedom win,
　　It aches in loneliness — is ill at peace
As the break-covert blood-hounds of such sin:
　　They dipp'd their swords in the water, and did tease
Their horses homeward, with convulsed spur,
Each richer by his being a murderer.

XXIX

They told their sister how, with sudden speed,
　　Lorenzo had ta'en ship for foreign lands,
Because of some great urgency and need
　　In their affairs, requiring trusty hands.
Poor Girl! put on thy stifling widow's weed,
　　And 'scape at once from Hope's accursed bands;
To-day thou wilt not see him, nor to-morrow,
And the next day will be a day of sorrow.

XXX

She weeps alone for pleasures not to be;
　　Sorely she wept until the night came on,
And then, instead of love, O misery!
　　She brooded o'er the luxury alone:
His image in the dusk she seem'd to see,
　　And to the silence made a gentle moan,
Spreading her perfect arms upon the air,
And on her couch low murmuring 'Where? O where?'

XLIII

When the full morning came, she had devised
　　How she might secret to the forest hie;
How she might find the clay, so dearly prized,
　　And sing to it one latest lullaby;

How her short absence might be unsurmised,
  While she the inmost of the dream would try.
Resolv'd, she took with her an aged nurse,
And went into that dismal forest-hearse.

XLIV

See, as they creep along the river side,
  How she doth whisper to that aged Dame,
And, after looking round the champaign wide,
  Shows her a knife. — 'What feverous hectic flame
'Burns in thee, child? — What good can thee betide,
  'That thou should'st smile again?' — The evening came,
And they had found Lorenzo's earthy bed;
The flint was there, the berries at his head.

XLV

Who hath not loiter'd in a green church-yard,
  And let his spirit, like a demon-mole,
Work through the clayey soil and gravel hard,
  To see scull, coffin'd bones, and funeral stole;
Pitying each form that hungry Death hath marr'd,
  And filling it once more with human soul?
Ah! this is holiday to what was felt
When Isabella by Lorenzo knelt.

XLVI

She gaz'd into the fresh-thrown mould, as though
  One glance did fully all its secrets tell;
Clearly she saw, as other eyes would know
  Pale limbs at bottom of a crystal well;
Upon the murderous spot she seem'd to grow,
  Like to a native lily of the dell:
Then with her knife, all sudden, she began
To dig more fervently than misers can.

59

XLVII

Soon she turn'd up a soiled glove, whereon
  Her silk had play'd in purple phantasies,
She kiss'd it with a lip more chill than stone,
  And put it in her bosom, where it dries
And freezes utterly unto the bone
  Those dainties made to still an infant's cries:
Then 'gan she work again; nor stay'd her care,
But to throw back at times her veiling hair.

XLVIII

That old nurse stood beside her wondering,
  Until her heart felt pity to the core
At sight of such a dismal labouring,
  And so she kneeled, with her locks all hoar,
And put her lean hands to the horrid thing:
  Three hours they labour'd at this travail sore;
At last they felt the kernel of the grave,
And Isabella did not stamp and rave.

XLIX

Ah! wherefore all this wormy circumstance?
  Why linger at the yawning tomb so long?
O for the gentleness of old Romance,
  The simple plaining of a minstrel's song!
Fair reader, at the old tale take a glance,
  For here, in truth, it doth not well belong
To speak: — O turn thee to the very tale,
And taste the music of that vision pale.

L

With duller steel than the Perséan sword
  They cut away no formless monster's head,
But one, whose gentleness did well accord
  With death, as life. The ancient harps have said,

Love never dies, but lives, immortal Lord:
    If Love impersonate was ever dead,
Pale Isabella kiss'd it, and low moan'd.
'Twas love; cold, — dead indeed, but not dethroned.

LI

In anxious secrecy they took it home,
    And then the prize was all for Isabel:
She calm'd its wild hair with a golden comb,
    And all around each eye's sepulchral cell
Pointed each fringed lash; the smeared loam
    With tears, as chilly as a dripping well,
She drench'd away: — and still she comb'd, and kept
Sighing all day — and still she kiss'd, and wept.

LII

Then in a silken scarf, — sweet with the dews
    Of precious flowers pluck'd in Araby,
And divine liquids come with odorous ooze
    Through the cold serpent-pipe refreshfully, —
She wrapp'd it up; and for its tomb did choose
    A garden-pot, wherein she laid it by,
And cover'd it with mould, and o'er it set
Sweet basil, which her tears kept ever wet.

LIII

And she forgot the stars, the moon, and sun,
    And she forgot the blue above the trees,
And she forgot the dells where waters run,
    And she forgot the chilly autumn breeze;
She had no knowledge when the day was done,
    And the new morn she saw not: but in peace
Hung over her sweet basil evermore,
And moisten'd it with tears unto the core.

61

The Eve of St Agnes

I

St. Agnes' Eve — Ah, bitter chill it was!
The owl, for all his feathers, was a-cold;
The hare limp'd trembling through the frozen grass,
And silent was the flock in woolly fold:
Numb were the Beadsman's fingers, while he told
His rosary, and while his frosted breath,
Like pious incense from a censer old,
Seem'd taking flight for heaven, without a death,
Past the sweet Virgin's picture, while his prayer he saith.

II

His prayer he saith, this patient, holy man;
Then takes his lamp, and riseth from his knees,
And back returneth, meagre, barefoot, wan,
Along the chapel aisle by slow degrees:
The sculptur'd dead, on each side, seem to freeze,
Emprison'd in black, purgatorial rails:
Knights, ladies, praying in dumb orat'ries,
He passeth by; and his weak spirit fails
To think how they may ache in icy hoods and mails.

III

Northward he turneth through a little door,
And scarce three steps, ere Music's golden tongue
Flatter'd to tears this aged man and poor;
But no — already had his deathbell rung;
The joys of all his life were said and sung:
His was harsh penance on St. Agnes' Eve:
Another way he went, and soon among
Rough ashes sat he for his soul's reprieve,
And all night kept awake, for sinners' sake to grieve.

IV

That ancient Beadsman heard the prelude soft;
And so it chanc'd, for many a door was wide,
From hurry to and fro. Soon, up aloft,
The silver, snarling trumpets 'gan to chide:
The level chambers, ready with their pride,
Were glowing to receive a thousand guests:
The carved angels, ever eager-eyed,
Star'd, where upon their heads the cornice rests,
With hair blown back, and wings put cross-wise on their breasts.

V

At length burst in the argent revelry,
With plume, tiara, and all rich array,
Numerous as shadows haunting fairily
The brain, new stuff'd, in youth, with triumphs gay
Of old romance. These let us wish away,
And turn, sole-thoughted, to one Lady there,
Whose heart had brooded, all that wintry day,
On love, and wing'd St. Agnes' saintly care,
As she had heard old dames full many times declare.

VI

They told her how, upon St. Agnes' Eve,
Young virgins might have visions of delight,
And soft adorings from their loves receive
Upon the honey'd middle of the night,
If ceremonies due they did aright;
As, supperless to bed they must retire,
And couch supine their beauties, lily white;
Nor look behind, nor sideways, but require
Of Heaven with upward eyes for all that they desire.

Full of this whim was thoughtful Madeline:
The music, yearning like a God in pain,
She scarcely heard: her maiden eyes divine,
Fix'd on the floor, saw many a sweeping train
Pass by — she heeded not at all: in vain
Came many a tiptoe, amorous cavalier,
And back retir'd; not cool'd by high disdain,
But she saw not: her heart was otherwhere:
She sigh'd for Agnes' dreams, the sweetest of the year.

She danc'd along with vague, regardless eyes,
Anxious her lips, her breathing quick and short:
The hallow'd hour was near at hand: she sighs
Amid the timbrels, and the throng'd resort
Of whisperers in anger, or in sport;
'Mid looks of love, defiance, hate, and scorn,
Hoodwink'd with faery fancy; all amort,
Save to St. Agnes and her lambs unshorn,
And all the bliss to be before to-morrow morn.

So, purposing each moment to retire,
She linger'd still. Meantime, across the moors,
Had come young Porphyro, with heart on fire
For Madeline. Beside the portal doors,
Buttress'd from moonlight, stands he, and implores
All saints to give him sight of Madeline,
But for one moment in the tedious hours,
That he might gaze and worship all unseen;
Perchance speak, kneel, touch, kiss — in sooth such things have
    been.

X

He ventures in: let not buzz'd whisper tell:
All eyes be muffled, or a hundred swords
Will storm his heart, Love's fev'rous citadel:
For him, those chambers held barbarian hordes,
Hyena foemen, and hot-blooded lords,
Whose very dogs would execrations howl
Against his lineage: not one breast affords
Him any mercy, in that mansion foul,
Save one old beldame, weak in body and in soul.

XI

Ah, happy chance! the aged creature came,
Shuffling along with ivory-headed wand,
To where he stood, hid from the torch's flame,
Behind a broad hall-pillar, far beyond
The sound of merriment and chorus bland:
He startled her; but soon she knew his face,
And grasp'd his fingers in her palsied hand,
Saying, 'Mercy, Porphyro! hie thee from this place;
'They are all here to-night, the whole blood-thirsty race!

XII

'Get hence! get hence! there's dwarfish Hildebrand;
'He had a fever late, and in the fit
'He cursed thee and thine, both house and land:
'Then there's that old Lord Maurice, not a whit
'More tame for his gray hairs — Alas me! flit!
'Flit like a ghost away.' — 'Ah, Gossip dear,
'We're safe enough; here in this arm-chair sit,
'And tell me how' — 'Good Saints! not here, not here;
'Follow me, child, or else these stones will be thy bier.'

XIII

He follow'd through a lowly arched way,
Brushing the cobwebs with his lofty plume,
And as she mutter'd 'Well-a — well-a-day!'
He found him in a little moonlight room,
Pale, lattic'd, chill, and silent as a tomb.
'Now tell me where is Madeline,' said he,
'O tell me, Angela, by the holy loom
'Which none but secret sisterhood may see,
'When they St. Agnes' wool are weaving piously.'

XIV

'St. Agnes! Ah! it is St. Agnes' Eve —
'Yet men will murder upon holy days:
'Thou must hold water in a witch's sieve,
'And be liege-lord of all the Elves and Fays,
'To venture so: it fills me with amaze
'To see thee, Porphyro! — St. Agnes' Eve!
'God's help! my lady fair the conjuror plays
'This very night: good angels her deceive!
'But let me laugh awhile, I've mickle time to grieve.'

XV

Feebly she laugheth in the languid moon,
While Porphyro upon her face doth look,
Like puzzled urchin on an aged crone
Who keepeth clos'd a wond'rous riddle-book,
As spectacled she sits in chimney nook.
But soon his eyes grew brilliant, when she told
His lady's purpose; and he scarce could brook
Tears, at the thought of those enchantments cold
And Madeline asleep in lap of legends old.

XVI

Sudden a thought came like a full-blown rose,
Flushing his brow, and in his pained heart
Made purple riot: then doth he propose
A stratagem, that makes the beldame start:
'A cruel man and impious thou art:
'Sweet lady, let her pray, and sleep, and dream
'Alone with her good angels, far apart
'From wicked men like thee. Go, go!—I deem
'Thou canst not surely be the same that thou didst seem.'

XVII

'I will not harm her, by all saints I swear,'
Quoth Porphyro: 'O may I ne'er find grace
'When my weak voice shall whisper its last prayer,
'If one of her soft ringlets I displace,
'Or look with ruffian passion in her face:
'Good Angela, believe me by these tears;
'Or I will, even in a moment's space,
'Awake, with horrid shout, my foemen's ears,
'And beard them, though they be more fang'd than wolves and
    bears.'

XVIII

'Ah! why wilt thou affright a feeble soul?
'A poor, weak, palsy-stricken, churchyard thing,
'Whose passing-bell may ere the midnight toll;
'Whose prayers for thee, each morn and evening,
'Were never miss'd.'—Thus plaining, doth she bring
A gentler speech from burning Porphyro;
So woful, and of such deep sorrowing,
That Angela gives promise she will do
Whatever he shall wish, betide her weal or woe.

67

XIX

Which was, to lead him, in close secrecy,
Even to Madeline's chamber, and there hide
Him in a closet, of such privacy
That he might see her beauty unespied,
And win perhaps that night a peerless bride,
While legion'd fairies pac'd the coverlet,
And pale enchantment held her sleepy-eyed.
Never on such a night have lovers met,
Since Merlin paid his Demon all the monstrous debt.

XX

'It shall be as thou wishest,' said the Dame:
'All cates and dainties shall be stored there
'Quickly on this feast-night: by the tambour frame
'Her own lute thou wilt see: no time to spare,
'For I am slow and feeble, and scarce dare
'On such a catering trust my dizzy head.
'Wait here, my child, with patience; kneel in prayer
'The while: Ah! thou must needs the lady wed,
'Or may I never leave my grave among the dead.'

XXI

So saying, she hobbled off with busy fear.
The lover's endless minutes slowly pass'd;
The dame return'd, and whisper'd in his ear
To follow her; with aged eyes aghast
From fright of dim espial. Safe at last,
Through many a dusky gallery, they gain
The maiden's chamber, silken, hush'd, and chaste;
Where Porphyro took covert, pleas'd amain.
His poor guide hurried back with agues in her brain.

XXII

Her falt'ring hand upon the balustrade,
Old Angela was feeling for the stair,
When Madeline, St. Agnes' charmed maid,
Rose, like a mission'd spirit, unaware:
With silver taper's light, and pious care,
She turn'd, and down the aged gossip led
To a safe level matting. Now prepare,
Young Porphyro, for gazing on that bed;
She comes, she comes again, like ring-dove fray'd and fled.

XXIII

Out went the taper as she hurried in;
Its little smoke, in pallid moonshine, died:
She clos'd the door, she panted, all akin
To spirits of the air, and visions wide:
No uttered syllable, or, woe betide!
But to her heart, her heart was voluble,
Paining with eloquence her balmy side;
As though a tongueless nightingale should swell
Her throat in vain, and die, heart-stifled, in her dell.

XXIV

A casement high and triple-arch'd there was,
All garlanded with carven imag'ries
Of fruits, and flowers, and bunches of knot-grass,
And diamonded with panes of quaint device,
Innumerable of stains and splendid dyes,
As are the tiger-moth's deep-damask'd wings;
And in the midst, 'mong thousand heraldries,
And twilight saints, and dim emblazonings,
A shielded scutcheon blush'd with blood of queens and kings.

XXV

Full on this casement shone the wintry moon,
And threw warm gules on Madeline's fair breast,
As down she knelt for heaven's grace and boon;
Rose-bloom fell on her hands, together prest,
And on her silver cross soft amethyst,
And on her hair a glory, like a saint:
She seem'd a splendid angel, newly drest,
Save wings, for heaven: — Porphyro grew faint:
She knelt, so pure a thing, so free from mortal taint.

XXVI

Anon his heart revives: her vespers done,
Of all its wreathed pearls her hair she frees;
Unclasps her warmed jewels one by one;
Loosens her fragrant boddice; by degrees
Her rich attire creeps rustling to her knees:
Half-hidden, like a mermaid in sea-weed,
Pensive awhile she dreams awake, and sees,
In fancy, fair St. Agnes in her bed,
But dares not look behind, or all the charm is fled.

XXVII

Soon, trembling in her soft and chilly nest,
In sort of wakeful swoon, perplex'd she lay,
Until the poppied warmth of sleep oppress'd
Her soothed limbs, and soul fatigued away;
Flown, like a thought, until the morrow-day;
Blissfully haven'd both from joy and pain;
Clasp'd like a missal where swart Paynims pray;
Blinded alike from sunshine and from rain,
As though a rose should shut, and be a bud again.

70

XXVIII

Stol'n to this paradise, and so entranced,
Porphyro gazed upon her empty dress,
And listen'd to her breathing, if it chanced
To wake into a slumberous tenderness;
Which when he heard, that minute did he bless,
And breath'd himself: then from the closet crept,
Noiseless as fear in a wide wilderness,
And over the hush'd carpet, silent, stept,
And 'tween the curtains peep'd, where, lo! — how fast she slept.

XXIX

Then by the bed-side, where the faded moon
Made a dim, silver twilight, soft he set
A table, and, half anguish'd, threw thereon
A cloth of woven crimson, gold, and jet: —
O for some drowsy Morphean amulet!
The boisterous, midnight, festive clarion,
The kettle-drum, and far-heard clarionet,
Affray his ears, though but in dying tone: —
The hall door shuts again, and all the noise is gone.

XXX

And still she slept an azure-lidded sleep,
In blanched linen, smooth, and lavender'd,
While he from forth the closet brought a heap
Of candied apple, quince, and plum, and gourd
With jellies soother than the creamy curd,
And lucent syrops, tinct with cinnamon;
Manna and dates, in argosy transferr'd
From Fez; and spiced dainties, every one,
From silken Samarcand to cedar'd Lebanon.

XXXI

These delicates he heap'd with glowing hand
On golden dishes and in baskets bright
Of wreathed silver: sumptuous they stand
In the retired quiet of the night,
Filling the chilly room with perfume light. —
'And now, my love, my seraph fair, awake!
'Thou art my heaven, and I thine eremite:
'Open thine eyes, for meek St. Agnes' sake,
'Or I shall drowse beside thee, so my soul doth ache.'

XXXII

Thus whispering, his warm, unnerved arm
Sank in her pillow. Shaded was her dream
By the dusk curtains: — 'twas a midnight charm
Impossible to melt as iced stream:
The lustrous salvers in the moonlight gleam;
Broad golden fringe upon the carpet lies:
It seem'd he never, never could redeem
From such a stedfast spell his lady's eyes;
So mus'd awhile, entoil'd in woofed phantasies.

XXXIII

Awakening up, he took her hollow lute, —
Tumultuous, — and, in chords that tenderest be,
He play'd an ancient ditty, long since mute,
In Provence call'd, 'La belle dame sans mercy:'
Close to her ear touching the melody; —
Wherewith disturb'd, she utter'd a soft moan:
He ceased — she panted quick — and suddenly
Her blue affrayed eyes wide open shone:
Upon his knees he sank, pale as smooth-sculptured stone.

XXXIV

Her eyes were open, but she still beheld,
Now wide awake, the vision of her sleep:
There was a painful change, that nigh expell'd
The blisses of her dream so pure and deep
At which fair Madeline began to weep,
And moan forth witless words with many a sigh;
While still her gaze on Porphyro would keep;
Who knelt, with joined hands and piteous eye,
Fearing to move or speak, she look'd so dreamingly.

XXXV

'Ah, Porphyro!' said she, 'but even now
'Thy voice was at sweet tremble in mine ear,
'Made tuneable with every sweetest vow;
'And those sad eyes were spiritual and clear:
'How chang'd thou art! how pallid, chill, and drear!
'Give me that voice again, my Porphyro,
'Those looks immortal, those complainings dear!
'Oh leave me not in this eternal woe,
'For if thou diest, my Love, I know not where to go.'

XXXVI

Beyond a mortal man impassion'd far
At these voluptuous accents, he arose,
Ethereal, flush'd, and like a throbbing star
Seen mid the sapphire heaven's deep repose
Into her dream he melted, as the rose
Blendeth its odour with the violet, —
Solution sweet: meantime the frost-wind blows
Like Love's alarum pattering the sharp sleet
Against the window-panes; St. Agnes' moon hath set.

XXXVII

'Tis dark: quick pattereth the flaw-blown sleet:
'This is no dream, my bride, my Madeline!'
'Tis dark: the iced gusts still rave and beat:
'No dream, alas! alas! and woe is mine!
'Porphyro will leave me here to fade and pine. —
'Cruel! what traitor could thee hither bring?
'I curse not, for my heart is lost in thine
'Though thou forsakest a deceived thing; —
'A dove forlorn and lost with sick unpruned wing.'

XXXVIII

'My Madeline! sweet dreamer! lovely bride!
'Say, may I be for aye thy vassal blest?
'Thy beauty's shield, heart-shap'd and vermeil dyed?
'Ah, silver shrine, here will I take my rest
'After so many hours of toil and quest,
'A famish'd pilgrim, — saved by miracle.
'Though I have found, I will not rob thy nest
'Saving of thy sweet self; if thou think'st well
'To trust, fair Madeline, to no rude infidel.'

XXXIX

'Hark! 'tis an elfin-storm from faery land,
'Of haggard seeming, but a boon indeed:
'Arise — arise! the morning is at hand; —
'The bloated wassaillers will never heed: —
'Let us away, my love, with happy speed;
'There are no ears to hear, or eyes to see, —
'Drown'd all in Rhenish and the sleepy mead:
'Awake! arise! my love, and fearless be,
'For o'er the southern moors I have a home for thee.'

She hurried at his words, beset with fears,
For there were sleeping dragons all around,
At glaring watch, perhaps, with ready spears —
Down the wide stairs a darkling way they found. —
In all the house was heard no human sound.
A chain-droop'd lamp was flickering by each door;
The arras, rich with horseman, hawk, and hound,
Flutter'd in the besieging wind's uproar;
And the long carpets rose along the gusty floor.

XLI

They glide, like phantoms, into the wide hall;
Like phantoms, to the iron porch, they glide;
Where lay the Porter, in uneasy sprawl,
With a huge empty flaggon by his side:
The wakeful bloodhound rose, and shook his hide,
But his sagacious eye an inmate owns:
By one, and one, the bolts full easy slide: —
The chains lie silent on the footworn stones; —
The key turns, and the door upon its hinges groans.

XLII

And they are gone: ay, ages long ago
These lovers fled away into the storm.
That night the Baron dreamt of many a woe,
And all his warrior-guests, with shade and form
Of witch, and demon, and large coffin-worm,
Were long be-nightmar'd. Angela the old
Died palsy-twitch'd, with meagre face deform;
The Beadsman, after thousand aves told,
For aye unsought for slept among his ashes cold.

Ode to a Nightingale

I

My heart aches, and a drowsy numbness pains
  My sense, as though of hemlock I had drunk,
Or emptied some dull opiate to the drains
  One minute past, and Lethe-wards had sunk:
'Tis not through envy of thy happy lot,
  But being too happy in thine happiness, —
    That thou, light-winged Dryad of the trees,
      In some melodious plot
Of beechen green, and shadows numberless,
  Singest of summer in full-throated ease.

2

O, for a draught of vintage! that hath been
  Cool'd a long age in the deep-delved earth,
Tasting of Flora and the country green,
  Dance, and Provençal song, and sunburnt mirth!
O for a beaker full of the warm South,
  Full of the true, the blushful Hippocrene,
    With beaded bubbles winking at the brim,
      And purple-stained mouth;
That I might drink, and leave the world unseen,
  And with thee fade away into the forest dim:

3

Fade far away, dissolve, and quite forget
  What thou among the leaves hast never known,
The weariness, the fever, and the fret
  Here, where men sit and hear each other groan;
Where palsy shakes a few, sad, last gray hairs,
  Where youth grows pale, and spectre-thin, and dies;
    Where but to think is to be full of sorrow
      And leaden-eyed despairs,
Where Beauty cannot keep her lustrous eyes,
  Or new Love pine at them beyond to-morrow.

4

Away! away! for I will fly to thee,
  Not charioted by Bacchus and his pards,
But on the viewless wings of Poesy,
  Though the dull brain perplexes and retards:
Already with thee! tender is the night,
  And haply the Queen-Moon is on her throne,
    Cluster'd around by all her starry Fays;
      But here there is no light,
  Save what from heaven is with the breezes blown
    Through verdurous glooms and winding mossy ways.

5

I cannot see what flowers are at my feet,
  Nor what soft incense hangs upon the boughs,
But, in embalmed darkness, guess each sweet
  Wherewith the seasonable month endows
The grass, the thicket, and the fruit-tree wild;
  White hawthorn, and the pastoral eglantine;
    Fast fading violets cover'd up in leaves;
      And mid-May's eldest child,
  The coming musk-rose, full of dewy wine,
    The murmurous haunt of flies on summer eves.

6

Darkling I listen; and, for many a time
  I have been half in love with easeful Death,
Call'd him soft names in many a mused rhyme,
  To take into the air my quiet breath;
Now more than ever seems it rich to die,
  To cease upon the midnight with no pain,
    While thou art pouring forth thy soul abroad
      In such an ecstasy!
  Still wouldst thou sing, and I have ears in vain —
    To thy high requiem become a sod.

7

Thou wast not born for death, immortal Bird!
  No hungry generations tread thee down;
The voice I hear this passing night was heard
  In ancient days by emperor and clown:
Perhaps the self-same song that found a path
  Through the sad heart of Ruth, when, sick for home,
    She stood in tears amid the alien corn;
      The same that oft-times hath
  Charm'd magic casements, opening on the foam
  Of perilous seas, in faery lands forlorn.

8

Forlorn! the very word is like a bell
  To toll me back from thee to my sole self!
Adieu! the fancy cannot cheat so well
  As she is fam'd to do, deceiving elf.
Adieu! adieu! thy plaintive anthem fades
  Past the near meadows, over the still stream,
    Up the hill-side; and now 'tis buried deep
      In the next valley-glades:
  Was it a vision, or a waking dream?
  Fled is that music:— Do I wake or sleep?

Ode on a Grecian Urn

I

Thou still unravish'd bride of quietness,
  Thou foster-child of silence and slow time,
Sylvan historian, who canst thus express
  A flowery tale more sweetly than our rhyme:
What leaf-fring'd legend haunts about thy shape
  Of deities or mortals, or of both,

In Tempe or the dales of Arcady?
What men or gods are these? What maidens loth?
What mad pursuit? What struggle to escape?
What pipes and timbrels? What wild ecstasy?

2

Heard melodies are sweet, but those unheard
  Are sweeter; therefore, ye soft pipes, play on;
Not to the sensual ear, but, more endear'd,
  Pipe to the spirit ditties of no tone:
Fair youth, beneath the trees, thou canst not leave
  Thy song, nor ever can those trees be bare;
    Bold Lover, never, never canst thou kiss,
Though winning near the goal — yet, do not grieve;
  She cannot fade, though thou hast not thy bliss,
    For ever wilt thou love, and she be fair!

3

Ah, happy, happy boughs! that cannot shed
  Your leaves, nor ever bid the Spring adieu;
And, happy melodist, unwearied,
  For ever piping songs for ever new;
More happy love! more happy, happy love!
  For ever warm and still to be enjoy'd,
    For ever panting, and for ever young;
All breathing human passion far above,
  That leaves a heart high-sorrowful and cloy'd,
    A burning forehead, and a parching tongue.

4

Who are these coming to the sacrifice?
  To what green altar, O mysterious priest,
Lead'st thou that heifer lowing at the skies,
  And all her silken flanks with garlands drest?
What little town by river or sea shore,
  Or mountain-built with peaceful citadel,

Is emptied of this folk, this pious morn?
And, little town, thy streets for evermore
    Will silent be; and not a soul to tell
    Why thou art desolate, can e'er return.

5

O Attic shape! Fair attitude! with brede
    Of marble men and maidens overwrought,
With forest branches and the trodden weed;
    Thou, silent form, dost tease us out of thought
As doth eternity: Cold Pastoral!
    When old age shall this generation waste,
        Thou shalt remain, in midst of other woe
Than ours, a friend to man, to whom thou say'st,
    Beauty is truth, truth beauty, — that is all
        Ye know on earth, and all ye need to know.

Ode to Psyche

O Goddess! hear these tuneless numbers, wrung
    By sweet enforcement and remembrance dear,
And pardon that thy secrets should be sung
    Even into thine own soft-conched ear:
Surely I dreamt to-day, or did I see
    The winged Psyche with awaken'd eyes?
I wander'd in a forest thoughtlessly,
    And, on the sudden, fainting with surprise,
Saw two fair creatures, couched side by side
    In deepest grass, beneath the whisp'ring roof
        Of leaves and trembled blossoms, where there ran
            A brooklet, scarce espied:
'Mid hush'd, cool-rooted flowers, fragrant-eyed,
    Blue, silver-white, and budded Tyrian,
They lay calm-breathing on the bedded grass;

80

Their arms embraced, and their pinions too;
  Their lips touch'd not, but had not bid adieu,
As if disjoined by soft-handed slumber,
And ready still past kisses to outnumber
  At tender eye-dawn of aurorean love:
      The winged boy I knew;
But who wast thou, O happy, happy dove?
      His Psyche true!

O latest born and loveliest vision far
  Of all Olympus' faded hierarchy!
Fairer than Phœbe's sapphire-region'd star,
  Or Vesper, amorous glow-worm of the sky;
Fairer than these, though temple thou hast none,
    Nor altar heap'd with flowers;
Nor virgin-choir to make delicious moan
    Upon the midnight hours;
No voice, no lute, no pipe, no incense sweet
  From chain-swung censer teeming;
No shrine, no grove, no oracle, no heat
  Of pale-mouth'd prophet dreaming.

O brightest! though too late for antique vows,
  Too, too late for the fond believing lyre,
When holy were the haunted forest boughs,
  Holy the air, the water, and the fire;
Yet even in these days so far retir'd
  From happy pieties, thy lucent fans,
  Fluttering among the faint Olympians,
I see, and sing, by my own eyes inspired.
So let me be thy choir, and make a moan
    Upon the midnight hours;
Thy voice, thy lute, thy pipe, thy incense sweet
  From swinged censer teeming;
Thy shrine, thy grove, thy oracle, thy heat
  Of pale-mouth'd prophet dreaming.

Yes, I will be thy priest, and build a fane
    In some untrodden region of my mind,
Where branched thoughts, new grown with pleasant pain,
    Instead of pines shall murmur in the wind:
Far, far around shall those dark-cluster'd trees
    Fledge the wild-ridged mountains steep by steep;
And there by zephyrs, streams, and birds, and bees,
    The moss-lain Dryads shall be lull'd to sleep;
And in the midst of this wide quietness
A rosy sanctuary will I dress
With the wreath'd trellis of a working brain,
    With buds, and bells, and stars without a name,
With all the gardener Fancy e'er could feign,
    Who breeding flowers, will never breed the same:
And there shall be for thee all soft delight
    That shadowy thought can win,
A bright torch, and a casement ope at night,
    To let the warm Love in!

Ode: 'Bards of Passion and of Mirth'

Bards of Passion and of Mirth,
Ye have left your souls on earth!
Have ye souls in heaven too,
Double-lived in regions new?
Yes, and those of heaven commune
With the spheres of sun and moon;
With the noise of fountains wond'rous,
And the parle of voices thund'rous;
With the whisper of heaven's trees
And one another, in soft ease
Seated on Elysian lawns
Brows'd by none but Dian's fawns
Underneath large blue-bells tented,
Where the daisies are rose-scented,

And the rose herself has got
Perfume which on earth is not;
Where the nightingale doth sing
Not a senseless, tranced thing,
But divine melodious truth;
Philosophic numbers smooth;
Tales and golden histories
Of heaven and its mysteries.

    Thus ye live on high, and then
On the earth ye live again;
And the souls ye left behind you
Teach us, here, the way to find you,
Where your other souls are joying,
Never slumber'd, never cloying.
Here, your earth-born souls still speak
To mortals, of their little week;
Of their sorrows and delights;
Of their passions and their spites;
Of their glory and their shame;
What does strengthen and what maim.
Thus ye teach us, every day,
Wisdom, though fled far away.

    Bards of Passion and of Mirth,
Ye have left your souls on earth!
Ye have souls in heaven too,
Double-lived in regions new!

Ode on Melancholy

I

No, no, go not to Lethe, neither twist
  Wolf's-bane, tight-rooted, for its poisonous wine;
Nor suffer thy pale forehead to be kiss'd
  By nightshade, ruby grape of Proserpine;
Make not your rosary of yew-berries,
  Nor let the beetle, nor the death-moth be
    Your mournful Psyche, nor the downy owl
A partner in your sorrow's mysteries;
  For shade to shade will come too drowsily,
    And drown the wakeful anguish of the soul.

2

But when the melancholy fit shall fall
  Sudden from heaven like a weeping cloud,
That fosters the droop-headed flowers all,
  And hides the green hill in an April shroud;
Then glut thy sorrow on a morning rose,
  Or on the rainbow of the salt sand-wave,
    Or on the wealth of globed peonies;
Or if thy mistress some rich anger shows,
  Emprison her soft hand, and let her rave,
    And feed deep, deep upon her peerless eyes.

3

She dwells with Beauty — Beauty that must die;
  And Joy, whose hand is ever at his lips
Bidding adieu; and aching Pleasure nigh,
  Turning to poison while the bee-mouth sips:
Ay, in the very temple of Delight
  Veil'd Melancholy has her sovran shrine,
    Though seen of none save him whose strenuous tongue
Can burst Joy's grape against his palate fine;
  His soul shall taste the sadness of her might,
    And be among her cloudy trophies hung.

To Autumn

1

Season of mists and mellow fruitfulness,
  Close bosom-friend of the maturing sun;
Conspiring with him how to load and bless
  With fruit the vines that round the thatch-eves run;
To bend with apples the moss'd cottage-trees,
  And fill all fruit with ripeness to the core;
    To swell the gourd, and plump the hazel shells
With a sweet kernel; to set budding more,
  And still more, later flowers for the bees,
  Until they think warm days will never cease,
    For Summer has o'er-brimm'd their clammy cells.

2

Who hath not seen thee oft amid thy store?
  Sometimes whoever seeks abroad may find
Thee sitting careless on a granary floor,
  Thy hair soft-lifted by the winnowing wind;
Or on a half-reap'd furrow sound asleep,
  Drows'd with the fume of poppies, while thy hook
    Spares the next swath and all its twined flowers:
And sometimes like a gleaner thou dost keep
  Steady thy laden head across a brook;
  Or by a cyder-press, with patient look,
    Thou watchest the last oozings hours by hours.

3

Where are the songs of Spring? Ay, where are they?
  Think not of them, thou hast thy music too, —
While barred clouds bloom the soft-dying day,
  And touch the stubble-plains with rosy hue;
Then in a wailful choir the small gnats mourn
  Among the river shallows, borne aloft
    Or sinking as the light wind lives or dies;

And full-grown lambs loud bleat from hilly bourn;
    Hedge-crickets sing; and now with treble soft
The red-breast whistles from a garden-croft;
    And gathering swallows twitter in the skies.

Hyperion (Books 1 and 11)

A FRAGMENT

BOOK I

Deep in the shady sadness of a vale
Far sunken from the healthy breath of morn,
Far from the fiery noon, and eve's one star,
Sat gray-hair'd Saturn, quiet as a stone,
Still as the silence round about his lair;
Forest on forest hung above his head
Like cloud on cloud. No stir of air was there,
Not so much life as on a summer's day
Robs not one light seed from the feather'd grass,
But where the dead leaf fell, there did it rest.
A stream went voiceless by still deadened more
By reason of his fallen divinity
Spreading a shade: the Naiad 'mid her reeds
Press'd her cold finger closer to her lips.

    Along the margin-sand large foot-marks went,
No further than to where his feet had stray'd,
And slept there since. Upon the sodden ground
His old right hand lay nerveless, listless, dead,
Unsceptred; and his realmless eyes were closed;
While his bow'd head seem'd list'ning to the Earth,
His ancient mother, for some comfort yet.

It seem'd no force could wake him from his place;
But there came one, who with a kindred hand
Touch'd his wide shoulders, after bending low
With reverence, though to one who knew it not.
She was a Goddess of the infant world;
By her in stature the tall Amazon
Had stood a pigmy's height: she would have ta'en
Achilles by the hair and bent his neck;
Or with a finger stay'd Ixion's wheel.
Her face was large as that of Memphian sphinx,
Pedestal'd haply in a palace court,
When sages look'd to Egypt for their lore.
But oh! how unlike marble was that face:
How beautiful, if sorrow had not made
Sorrow more beautiful than Beauty's self.
There was a listening fear in her regard,
As if calamity had but begun;
As if the vanward clouds of evil days
Had spent their malice, and the sullen rear
Was with its stored thunder labouring up.
One hand she press'd upon that aching spot
Where beats the human heart, as if just there,
Though an immortal, she felt cruel pain:
The other upon Saturn's bended neck
She laid, and to the level of his ear
Leaning with parted lips, some words she spake
In solemn tenour and deep organ tone:
Some mourning words, which in our feeble tongue
Would come in these like accents; O how frail
To that large utterance of the early Gods!
'Saturn, look up! — though wherefore, poor old King?
'I have no comfort for thee, no not one:
'I cannot say, "O wherefore sleepest thou?"
'For heaven is parted from thee, and the earth
'Knows thee not, thus afflicted, for a God;
'And ocean too, with all its solemn noise,
'Has from thy sceptre pass'd; and all the air
'Is emptied of thine hoary majesty.

'Thy thunder, conscious of the new command,
'Rumbles reluctant o'er our fallen house;
'And thy sharp lightning in unpractised hands
'Scorches and burns our once serene domain.
'O aching time! O moments big as years!
'All as ye pass swell out the monstrous truth,
'And press it so upon our weary griefs
'That unbelief has not a space to breathe.
'Saturn, sleep on: — O thoughtless, why did I
'Thus violate thy slumbrous solitude?
'Why should I ope thy melancholy eyes?
'Saturn, sleep on! while at thy feet I weep.'

    As when, upon a tranced summer-night,
Those green-rob'd senators of mighty woods,
Tall oaks, branch-charmed by the earnest stars,
Dream, and so dream all night without a stir,
Save from one gradual solitary gust
Which comes upon the silence, and dies off,
As if the ebbing air had but one wave;
So came these words and went; the while in tears
She touch'd her fair large forehead to the ground,
Just where her fallen hair might be outspread
A soft and silken mat for Saturn's feet.
One moon, with alteration slow, had shed
Her silver seasons four upon the night,
And still these two were postured motionless,
Like natural sculpture in cathedral cavern;
The frozen God still couchant on the earth,
And the sad Goddess weeping at his feet:
Until at length old Saturn lifted up
His faded eyes, and saw his kingdom gone,
And all the gloom and sorrow of the place,
And that fair kneeling Goddess; and then spake,
As with a palsied tongue, and while his beard
Shook horrid with such aspen-malady:
'O tender spouse of gold Hyperion,
'Thea, I feel thee ere I see thy face;

'Look up, and let me see our doom in it;
'Look up, and tell me if this feeble shape
'Is Saturn's; tell me, if thou hear'st the voice
'Of Saturn; tell me, if this wrinkling brow,
'Naked and bare of its great diadem,
'Peers like the front of Saturn. Who had power
'To make me desolate? whence came the strength?
'How was it nurtur'd to such bursting forth,
'While Fate seem'd strangled in my nervous grasp?
'But it is so; and I am smother'd up,
'And buried from all godlike exercise
'Of influence benign on planets pale,
'Of admonitions to the winds and seas,
'Of peaceful sway above man's harvesting,
'And all those acts which Deity supreme
'Doth ease its heart of love in. — I am gone
'Away from my own bosom: I have left
'My strong identity, my real self,
'Somewhere between the throne, and where I sit
'Here on this spot of earth. Search, Thea, search!
'Open thine eyes eterne, and sphere them round
'Upon all space: space starr'd, and lorn of light;
'Space region'd with life-air; and barren void;
'Spaces of fire, and all the yawn of hell. —
'Search, Thea, search! and tell me, if thou seest
'A certain shape or shadow, making way
'With wings or chariot fierce to repossess
'A heaven he lost erewhile: it must — it must
'Be of ripe progress — Saturn must be King.
'Yes, there must be a golden victory;
'There must be Gods thrown down, and trumpets blown
'Of triumph calm, and hymns of festival
'Upon the gold clouds metropolitan,
'Voices of soft proclaim, and silver stir
'Of strings in hollow shells; and there shall be
'Beautiful things made new, for the surprise
'Of the sky-children; I will give command:
'Thea! Thea! Thea! where is Saturn?'

This passion lifted him upon his feet,
And made his hands to struggle in the air,
His Druid locks to shake and ooze with sweat,
His eyes to fever out, his voice to cease.
He stood, and heard not Thea's sobbing deep;
A little time, and then again he snatch'd
Utterance thus. — 'But cannot I create?
'Cannot I form? Cannot I fashion forth
'Another world, another universe,
'To overbear and crumble this to nought?
'Where is another Chaos? Where?' — That word
Found way unto Olympus, and made quake
The rebel three. — Thea was startled up,
And in her bearing was a sort of hope,
As thus she quick-voic'd spake, yet full of awe.

'This cheers our fallen house: come to our friends,
'O Saturn! come away, and give them heart;
'I know the covert, for thence came I hither.'
Thus brief; then with beseeching eyes she went
With backward footing through the shade a space:
He follow'd, and she turn'd to lead the way
Through aged boughs, that yielded like the mist
Which eagles cleave upmounting from their nest.

Meanwhile in other realms big tears were shed,
More sorrow like to this, and such like woe,
Too huge for mortal tongue or pen of scribe:
The Titans fierce, self-hid, or prison-bound,
Groan'd for the old allegiance once more,
And listen'd in sharp pain for Saturn's voice.
But one of the whole mammoth-brood still kept
His sov'reignty, and rule, and majesty; —
Blazing Hyperion on his orbed fire
Still sat, still snuff'd the incense, teeming up
From Man to the sun's God; yet unsecure:
For as among us mortals omens drear
Fright and perplex, so also shuddered he —

Not at dog's howl, or gloom-bird's hated screech,
Or the familiar visiting of one
Upon the first toll of his passing-bell,
Or prophesyings of the midnight lamp;
But horrors, portion'd to a giant nerve,
Oft made Hyperion ache. His palace bright
Bastion'd with pyramids of glowing gold,
And touch'd with shade of bronzed obelisks,
Glar'd a blood-red through all its thousand courts,
Arches, and domes, and fiery galleries;
And all its curtains of Aurorian clouds
Flush'd angerly: while sometimes eagle's wings,
Unseen before by Gods or wondering men,
Darken'd the place; and neighing steeds were heard,
Not heard before by Gods or wondering men.
Also, when he would taste the spicy wreaths
Of incense, breath'd aloft from sacred hills,
Instead of sweets, his ample palate took
Savour of poisonous brass and metal sick:
And so, when harbour'd in the sleepy west,
After the full completion of fair day, —
For rest divine upon exalted couch
And slumber in the arms of melody,
He pac'd away the pleasant hours of ease
With stride colossal, on from hall to hall;
While far within each aisle and deep recess,
His winged minions in close clusters stood,
Amaz'd and full of fear; like anxious men
Who on wide plains gather in panting troops,
When earthquakes jar their battlements and towers.
Even now, while Saturn, rous'd from icy trance,
Went step for step with Thea through the woods,
Hyperion, leaving twilight in the rear,
Came slope upon the threshold of the west;
Then, as was wont, his palace-door flew ope
In smoothest silence, save what solemn tubes,
Blown by the serious Zephyrs, gave of sweet
And wandering sounds, slow-breathed melodies;

And like a rose in vermeil tint and shape,
In fragrance soft, and coolness to the eye,
That inlet to severe magnificence
Stood full blown, for the God to enter in.

He enter'd, but he enter'd full of wrath;
His flaming robes stream'd out beyond his heels,
And gave a roar, as if of earthly fire,
That scar'd away the meek ethereal Hours
And made their dove-wings tremble. On he flared,
From stately nave to nave, from vault to vault,
Through bowers of fragrant and enwreathed light,
And diamond-paved lustrous long arcades,
Until he reach'd the great main cupola;
There standing fierce beneath, he stampt his foot,
And from the basements deep to the high towers
Jarr'd his own golden region; and before
The quavering thunder thereupon had ceas'd,
His voice leapt out, despite of godlike curb,
To this result: 'O dreams of day and night!
'O monstrous forms! O effigies of pain!
'O spectres busy in a cold, cold gloom!
'O lank-eared Phantoms of black-weeded pools!
'Why do I know ye? why have I seen ye? why
'Is my eternal essence thus distraught
'To see and to behold these horrors new?
'Saturn is fallen, am I too to fall?
'Am I to leave this haven of my rest,
'This cradle of my glory, this soft clime,
'This calm luxuriance of blissful light,
'These crystalline pavilions, and pure fanes,
'Of all my lucent empire? It is left
'Deserted, void, nor any haunt of mine.
'The blaze, the splendor, and the symmetry
'I cannot see — but darkness, death and darkness.
'Even here, into my centre of repose,
'The shady visions come to domineer,
'Insult, and blind, and stifle up my pomp. —

'Fall! — No, by Tellus and her briny robes!
'Over the fiery frontier of my realms
'I will advance a terrible right arm
'Shall scare that infant Thunderer, rebel Jove,
'And bid old Saturn take his throne again.' —
He spake, and ceas'd, the while a heavier threat
Held struggle with his throat but came not forth;
For as in theatres of crowded men
Hubbub increases more they call out 'Hush!'
So at Hyperion's words the Phantoms pale
Bestirr'd themselves, thrice horrible and cold;
And from the mirror'd level where he stood
A mist arose, as from a scummy marsh.
At this, through all his bulk an agony
Crept gradual, from the feet unto the crown,
Like a lithe serpent vast and muscular
Making slow way, with head and neck convuls'd
From over-strained might. Releas'd, he fled
To the eastern gates, and full six dewy hours
Before the dawn in season due should blush,
He breath'd fierce breath against the sleepy portals,
Clear'd them of heavy vapours, burst them wide
Suddenly on the ocean's chilly streams.
The planet orb of fire, whereon he rode
Each day from east to west the heavens through,
Spun round in sable curtaining of clouds;
Not therefore veiled quite, blindfold, and hid,
But ever and anon the glancing spheres,
Circles, and arcs, and broad-belting colure,
Glow'd through, and wrought upon the muffling dark
Sweet-shaped lightnings from the nadir deep
Up to the zenith, — hieroglyphics old,
Which sages and keen-eyed astrologers
Then living on the earth, with labouring thought
Won from the gaze of many centuries:
Now lost, save what we find on remnants huge
Of stone, or marble swart; their import gone,
Their wisdom long since fled. — Two wings this orb

Possess'd for glory, two fair argent wings,
Ever exalted at the God's approach
And now, from forth the gloom their plumes immense
Rose, one by one, till all outspreaded were;
While still the dazzling globe maintain'd eclipse,
Awaiting for Hyperion's command.
Fain would he have commanded, fain took throne
And bid the day begin, if but for change.
He might not: — No, though a primeval God:
The sacred seasons might not be disturb'd.
Therefore the operations of the dawn
Stay'd in their birth, even as here 'tis told.
Those silver wings expanded sisterly,
Eager to sail their orb; the porches wide
Open'd upon the dusk demesnes of night
And the bright Titan, phrenzied with new woes,
Unus'd to bend, by hard compulsion bent
His spirit to the sorrow of the time;
And all along a dismal rack of clouds,
Upon the boundaries of day and night,
He stretch'd himself in grief and radiance faint.
There as he lay, the Heaven with its stars
Look'd down on him with pity, and the voice
Of Cœlus, from the universal space,
Thus whisper'd low and solemn in his ear.
'O brightest of my children dear, earth-born
'And sky-engendered, Son of Mysteries
'All unrevealed even to the powers
'Which met at thy creating; at whose joys
'And palpitations sweet, and pleasures soft,
'I, Cœlus, wonder, how they came and whence;
'And at the fruits thereof what shapes they be,
'Distinct, and visible; symbols divine,
'Manifestations of that beauteous life
'Diffus'd unseen throughout eternal space:
'Of these new-form'd art thou, oh brightest child!
'Of these, thy brethren and the Goddesses!
'There is sad feud among ye, and rebellion

'Of son against his sire. I saw him fall,
'I saw my first-born tumbled from his throne!
'To me his arms were spread, to me his voice
'Found way from forth the thunders round his head!
'Pale wox I, and in vapours hid my face.
'Art thou, too, near such doom? vague fear there is:
'For I have seen my sons most unlike Gods.
'Divine ye were created, and divine
'In sad demeanour, solemn, undisturb'd,
'Unruffled, like high Gods, ye liv'd and ruled:
'Now I behold in you fear, hope, and wrath;
'Actions of rage and passion; even as
'I see them, on the mortal world beneath,
'In men who die. — This is the grief, O Son!
'Sad sign of ruin, sudden dismay, and fall!
'Yet do thou strive; as thou art capable,
'As thou canst move about, an evident God;
'And canst oppose to each malignant hour
'Ethereal presence: — I am but a voice;
'My life is but the life of winds and tides,
'No more than winds and tides can I avail: —
'But thou canst. — Be thou therefore in the van
'Of Circumstance; yea, seize the arrow's barb
'Before the tense string murmur. — To the earth!
'For there thou wilt find Saturn, and his woes.
'Meantime I will keep watch on thy bright sun,
'And of thy seasons be a careful nurse.' —
Ere half this region-whisper had come down,
Hyperion arose, and on the stars
Lifted his curved lids, and kept them wide
Until it ceas'd; and still he kept them wide:
And still they were the same bright, patient stars.
Then with a slow incline of his broad breast,
Like to a diver in the pearly seas,
Forward he stoop'd over the airy shore,
And plung'd all noiseless into the deep night.

BOOK II

Just at the self-same beat of Time's wide wings
Hyperion slid into the rustled air,
And Saturn gain'd with Thea that sad place
Where Cybele and the bruised Titans mourn'd.
It was a den where no insulting light
Could glimmer on their tears; where their own groans
They felt, but heard not, for the solid roar
Of thunderous waterfalls and torrents hoarse,
Pouring a constant bulk, uncertain where.
Crag jutting forth to crag, and rocks that seem'd
Ever as if just rising from a sleep,
Forehead to forehead held their monstrous horns;
And thus in thousand hugest phantasies
Made a fit roofing to this nest of woe.
Instead of thrones, hard flint they sat upon,
Couches of rugged stone, and slaty ridge
Stubborn'd with iron. All were not assembled:
Some chain'd in torture, and some wandering.
Cœus, and Gyges, and Briareüs,
Typhon, and Dolor, and Porphyrion,
With many more, the brawniest in assault,
Were pent in regions of laborious breath;
Dungeon'd in opaque element, to keep
Their clenched teeth still clench'd, and all their limbs
Lock'd up like veins of metal, crampt and screw'd;
Without a motion, save of their big hearts
Heaving in pain, and horribly convuls'd
With sanguine feverous boiling gurge of pulse.
Mnemosyne was straying in the world;
Far from her moon had Phœbe wandered;
And many else were free to roam abroad,
But for the main, here found they covert drear.
Scarce images of life, one here, one there,
Lay vast and edgeways; like a dismal cirque
Of Druid stones, upon a forlorn moor,
When the chill rain begins at shut of eve,

In dull November, and their chancel vault,
The Heaven itself, is blinded throughout night.
Each one kept shroud, nor to his neighbour gave
Or word, or look, or action of despair.
Creüs was one; his ponderous iron mace
Lay by him, and a shatter'd rib of rock
Told of his rage, ere he thus sank and pined.
Iäpetus another; in his grasp,
A serpent's plashy neck; its barbed tongue
Squeez'd from the gorge, and all its uncurl'd length
Dead; and because the creature could not spit
Its poison in the eyes of conquering Jove.
Next Cottus: prone he lay, chin uppermost,
As though in pain; for still upon the flint
He ground severe his skull, with open mouth
And eyes at horrid working. Nearest him
Asia, born of most enormous Caf,
Who cost her mother Tellus keener pangs,
Though feminine, than any of her sons:
More thought than woe was in her dusky face,
For she was prophesying of her glory;
And in her wide imagination stood
Palm-shaded temples, and high rival fanes,
By Oxus or in Ganges' sacred isles.
Even as Hope upon her anchor leans,
So leant she, not so fair, upon a tusk
Shed from the broadest of her elephants.
Above her, on a crag's uneasy shelve,
Upon his elbow rais'd, all prostrate else,
Shadow'd Enceladus; once tame and mild
As grazing ox unworried in the meads;
Now tiger-passion'd, lion-thoughted, wroth,
He meditated, plotted, and even now
Was hurling mountains in that second war,
Not long delay'd, that scar'd the younger Gods
To hide themselves in forms of beast and bird.
Not far hence Atlas; and beside him prone
Phorcus, the sire of Gorgons. Neighbour'd close

Oceanus, and Tethys, in whose lap
Sobb'd Clymene among her tangled hair.
In midst of all lay Themis, at the feet
Of Ops the queen; all clouded round from sight,
No shape distinguishable, more than when
Thick night confounds the pine-tops with the clouds:
And many else whose names may not be told.
For when the Muse's wings are air-ward spread,
Who shall delay her flight? And she must chaunt
Of Saturn, and his guide, who now had climb'd
With damp and slippery footing from a depth
More horrid still. Above a sombre cliff
Their heads appear'd, and up their stature grew
Till on the level height their steps found ease:
Then Thea spread abroad her trembling arms
Upon the precincts of this nest of pain,
And sidelong fix'd her eye on Saturn's face:
There saw she direst strife; the supreme God
At war with all the frailty of grief,
Of rage, of fear, anxiety, revenge,
Remorse, spleen, hope, but most of all despair.
Against these plagues he strove in vain; for Fate
Had pour'd a mortal oil upon his head,
A disanointing poison: so that Thea,
Affrighted, kept her still, and let him pass
First onwards in, among the fallen tribe.

    As with us mortal men, the laden heart
Is persecuted more, and fever'd more,
When it is nighing to the mournful house
Where other hearts are sick of the same bruise;
So Saturn, as he walk'd into the midst,
Felt faint, and would have sunk among the rest,
But that he met Enceladus's eye,
Whose mightiness, and awe of him, at once
Came like an inspiration; and he shouted,
'Titans, behold your God!' at which some groan'd;
Some started on their feet; some also shouted;

Some wept, some wail'd, all bow'd with reverence;
And Ops, uplifting her black folded veil,
Show'd her pale cheeks, and all her forehead wan,
Her eye-brows thin and jet, and hollow eyes.
There is a roaring in the bleak-grown pines
When Winter lifts his voice; there is a noise
Among immortals when a God gives sign,
With hushing finger, how he means to load
His tongue with the full weight of utterless thought,
With thunder, and with music, and with pomp:
Such noise is like the roar of bleak-grown pines;
Which, when it ceases in this mountain'd world,
No other sound succeeds; but ceasing here,
Among these fallen, Saturn's voice therefrom
Grew up like organ, that begins anew
Its strain, when other harmonies, stopt short,
Leave the dinn'd air vibrating silverly.
Thus grew it up — 'Not in my own sad breast,
'Which is its own great judge and searcher out,
'Can I find reason why ye should be thus:
'Not in the legends of the first of days,
'Studied from that old spirit-leaved book
'Which starry Uranus with finger bright
'Sav'd from the shores of darkness, when the waves
'Low-ebb'd still hid it up in shallow gloom; —
'And the which book ye know I ever kept
'For my firm-based footstool: — Ah, infirm!
'Not there, nor in sign, symbol, or portent
'Of element, earth, water, air, and fire, —
'At war, at peace, or inter-quarrelling
'One against one, or two, or three, or all
'Each several one against the other three,
'As fire with air loud warring when rain-floods
'Drown both, and press them both against earth's face.
'Where, finding sulphur, a quadruple wrath
'Unhinges the poor world; — not in that strife,
'Wherefrom I take strange lore, and read it deep,
'Can I find reason why ye should be thus:

'No, no-where can unriddle, though I search,
'And pore on Nature's universal scroll
'Even to swooning, why ye, Divinities,
'The first-born of all shap'd and palpable Gods,
'Should cower beneath what, in comparison,
'Is untremendous might. Yet ye are here,
'O'erwhelm'd, and spurn'd, and batter'd, ye are here!
'O Titans, shall I say "Arise!" — Ye groan:
'Shall I say "Crouch!" — Ye groan. What can I then?
'O Heaven wide! O unseen parent dear!
'What can I? Tell me, all ye brethren Gods,
'How we can war, how engine our great wrath!
'O speak your counsel now, for Saturn's ear
'Is all a-hunger'd. Thou, Oceanus,
'Ponderest high and deep; and in thy face
'I see, astonied, that severe content
'Which comes of thought and musing: give us help!'

     So ended Saturn; and the God of the Sea,
Sophist and sage, from no Athenian grove,
But cogitation in his watery shades,
Arose, with locks not oozy, and began,
In murmurs, which his first-endeavouring tongue
Caught infant-like from the far-foamed sands.
'O ye, whom wrath consumes! who, passion-stung,
'Writhe at defeat, and nurse your agonies!
'Shut up your senses, stifle up your ears,
'My voice is not a bellows unto ire.
'Yet listen, ye who will, whilst I bring proof
'How ye, perforce, must be content to stoop:
'And in the proof much comfort will I give,
'If ye will take that comfort in its truth.
'We fall by course of Nature's law, not force
'Of thunder, or of Jove. Great Saturn, thou
'Hast sifted well the atom-universe;
'But for this reason, that thou art the King,
'And only blind from sheer supremacy,
'One avenue was shaded from thine eyes,

'Through which I wandered to eternal truth.
'And first, as thou wast not the first of powers,
'So art thou not the last; it cannot be:
'Thou art not the beginning nor the end.
'From Chaos and parental Darkness came
'Light, the first fruits of that intestine broil,
'That sullen ferment, which for wondrous ends
'Was ripening in itself. The ripe hour came,
'And with it Light, and Light, engendering
'Upon its own producer, forthwith touch'd
'The whole enormous matter into Life.
'Upon that very hour, our parentage,
'The Heavens and the Earth, were manifest:
'Then thou first born, and we the giant race,
'Found ourselves ruling new and beauteous realms.
'Now comes the pain of truth, to whom 'tis pain;
'O folly! for to bear all naked truths,
'And to envisage circumstance, all calm,
'That is the top of sovereignty. Mark well!
'As Heaven and Earth are fairer, fairer far
'Than Chaos and blank Darkness, though once chiefs;
'And as we show beyond that Heaven and Earth
'In form and shape compact and beautiful,
'In will, in action free, companionship,
'And thousand other signs of purer life;
'So on our heels a fresh perfection treads,
'A power more strong in beauty, born of us
'And fated to excel us, as we pass
'In glory that old Darkness: nor are we
'Thereby more conquer'd, than by us the rule
'Of shapeless Chaos. Say, doth the dull soil
'Quarrel with the proud forests it hath fed,
'And feedeth still, more comely than itself?
'Can it deny the chiefdom of green groves?
'Or shall the tree be envious of the dove
'Because it cooeth, and hath snowy wings
'To wander wherewithal and find its joys?
'We are such forest-trees, and our fair boughs

'Have bred forth, not pale solitary doves,
'But eagles golden-feather'd, who do tower
'Above us in their beauty, and must reign
'In right thereof; for 'tis the eternal law
'That first in beauty should be first in might:
'Yea, by that law, another race may drive
'Our conquerors to mourn as we do now.
'Have ye beheld the young God of the Seas,
'My dispossessor? Have ye seen his face?
'Have ye beheld his chariot, foam'd along
'By noble winged creatures he hath made?
'I saw him on the calmed waters scud,
'With such a glow of beauty in his eyes,
'That it enforc'd me to bid sad farewell
'To all my empire: farewell sad I took,
'And hither came, to see how dolorous fate
'Had wrought upon ye; and how I might best
'Give consolation in this woe extreme.
'Receive the truth, and let it be your balm.'

    Whether through poz'd conviction, or disdain,
They guarded silence, when Oceanus
Left murmuring, what deepest thought can tell?
But so it was, none answer'd for a space,
Save one whom none regarded, Clymene;
And yet she answer'd not, only complain'd,
With hectic lips, and eyes up-looking mild,
Thus wording timidly among the fierce:
'O Father, I am here the simplest voice,
'And all my knowledge is that joy is gone,
'And this thing woe crept in among our hearts,
'There to remain for ever, as I fear:
'I would not bode of evil, if I thought
'So weak a creature could turn off the help
'Which by just right should come of mighty Gods;
'Yet let me tell my sorrow, let me tell
'Of what I heard, and how it made me weep,
'And know that we had parted from all hope.

'I stood upon a shore, a pleasant shore,
'Where a sweet clime was breathed from a land
'Of fragrance, quietness, and trees, and flowers.
'Full of calm joy it was, as I of grief;
'Too full of joy and soft delicious warmth;
'So that I felt a movement in my heart
'To chide, and to reproach that solitude
'With songs of misery, music of our woes;
'And sat me down, and took a mouthed shell
'And murmur'd into it, and made melody —
'O melody no more! for while I sang,
'And with poor skill let pass into the breeze
'The dull shell's echo, from a bowery strand
'Just opposite, an island of the sea,
'There came enchantment with the shifting wind,
'That did both drown and keep alive my ears.
'I threw my shell away upon the sand,
'And a wave fill'd it, as my sense was fill'd
'With that new blissful golden melody.
'A living death was in each gush of sounds,
'Each family of rapturous hurried notes,
'That fell, one after one, yet all at once,
'Like pearl beads dropping sudden from their string:
'And then another, then another strain,
'Each like a dove leaving its olive perch,
'With music wing'd instead of silent plumes,
'To hover round my head, and make me sick
'Of joy and grief at once. Grief overcame,
'And I was stopping up my frantic ears,
'When, past all hindrance of my trembling hands,
'A voice came sweeter, sweeter than all tune,
'And still it cried, "Apollo! young Apollo!
' "The morning-bright Apollo! young Apollo!"
'I fled, it follow'd me, and cried "Apollo!"
'O Father, and O Brethren, had ye felt
'Those pains of mine; O Saturn, hadst thou felt,
'Ye would not call this too indulged tongue
'Presumptuous, in thus venturing to be heard.'

So far her voice flow'd on, like timorous brook
That, lingering along a pebbled coast,
Doth fear to meet the sea: but sea it met,
And shudder'd; for the overwhelming voice
Of huge Enceladus swallow'd it in wrath:
The ponderous syllables, like sullen waves
In the half-glutted hollows of reef-rocks,
Came booming thus, while still upon his arm
He lean'd; not rising, from supreme contempt.
'Or shall we listen to the over-wise,
'Or to the over-foolish, Giant-Gods?
'Not thunderbolt on thunderbolt, till all
'That rebel Jove's whole armoury were spent,
'Not world on world upon these shoulders piled,
'Could agonize me more than baby-words
'In midst of this dethronement horrible.
'Speak! roar! shout! yell! ye sleepy Titans all.
'Do ye forget the blows, the buffets vile?
'Are ye not smitten by a youngling arm?
'Dost thou forget, sham Monarch of the Waves,
'Thy scalding in the seas? What, have I rous'd
'Your spleens with so few simple words as these?
'O joy! for now I see ye are not lost:
'O joy! for now I see a thousand eyes
'Wide-glaring for revenge!' — As this he said,
He lifted up his stature vast, and stood,
Still without intermission speaking thus:
'Now ye are flames, I'll tell you how to burn,
'And purge the ether of our enemies;
'How to feed fierce the crooked stings of fire,
'And singe away the swollen clouds of Jove,
'Stifling that puny essence in its tent.
'O let him feel the evil he hath done;
'For though I scorn Oceanus's lore,
'Much pain have I for more than loss of realms;
'The days of peace and slumberous calm are fled;
'Those days, all innocent of scathing war,
'When all the fair Existences of heaven

'Came open-eyed to guess what we would speak: —
'That was before our brows were taught to frown,
'Before our lips knew else but solemn sounds;
'That was before we knew the winged thing,
'Victory, might be lost, or might be won.
'And be ye mindful that Hyperion,
'Our brightest brother, still is undisgraced —
'Hyperion, lo! his radiance is here!'

  All eyes were on Enceladus's face,
And they beheld, while still Hyperion's name
Flew from his lips up to the vaulted rocks,
A pallid gleam across his features stern:
Not savage, for he saw full many a God
Wroth as himself. He look'd upon them all,
And in each face he saw a gleam of light,
But splendider in Saturn's, whose hoar locks
Shone like the bubbling foam about a keel
When the prow sweeps into a midnight cove.
In pale and silver silence they remain'd,
Till suddenly a splendour, like the morn,
Pervaded all the beetling gloomy steeps,
All the sad spaces of oblivion,
And every gulf, and every chasm old,
And every height, and every sullen depth,
Voiceless, or hoarse with loud tormented streams:
And all the everlasting cataracts,
And all the headlong torrents far and near,
Mantled before in darkness and huge shade,
Now saw the light and made it terrible.
It was Hyperion: — a granite peak
His bright feet touch'd, and there he stay'd to view
The misery his brilliance had betray'd
To the most hateful seeing of itself.
Golden his hair of short Numidian curl,
Regal his shape majestic, a vast shade
In midst of his own brightness, like the bulk
Of Memnon's image at the set of sun

To one who travels from the dusking East:
Sighs, too, as mournful as that Memnon's harp
He utter'd, while his hands contemplative
He press'd together, and in silence stood.
Despondence seiz'd again the fallen Gods
At sight of the dejected King of Day,
And many hid their faces from the light:
But fierce Enceladus sent forth his eyes
Among the brotherhood; and, at their glare,
Uprose Iäpetus, and Creüs too,
And Phorcus, sea-born, and together strode
To where he towered on his eminence.
There those four shouted forth old Saturn's name;
Hyperion from the peak loud answered, 'Saturn!'
Saturn sat near the Mother of the Gods,
In whose face was no joy, though all the Gods
Gave from their hollow throats the name of 'Saturn!'

The Fall of Hyperion (ll. 1–290)

CANTO I

Fanatics have their dreams, wherewith they weave
A paradise for a sect; the savage too
From forth the loftiest fashion of his sleep
Guesses at Heaven: pity these have not
Trac'd upon vellum or wild indian leaf
The shadows of melodious utterance.
But bare of laurel they live, dream and die;
For Poesy alone can tell her dreams,
With the fine spell of words alone can save
Imagination from the sable charm
And dumb enchantment. Who alive can say
'Thou art no Poet; mayst not tell thy dreams'?

Since every man whose soul is not a clod
Hath visions, and would speak, if he had lov'd
And been well nurtured in his mother tongue
Whether the dream now purposed to rehearse
Be Poet's or Fanatic's will be known
When this warm scribe my hand is in the grave.

   Methought I stood where trees of every clime,
Palm, myrtle, oak, and sycamore, and beech,
With Plantane, and spice blossoms, made a screen;
In neighbourhood of fountains, by the noise
Soft-showering in mine ears; and, by the touch
Of scent, not far from roses. Turning round,
I saw an arbour with a drooping roof
Of trellis vines, and bells, and larger blooms,
Like floral censers swinging light in air;
Before its wreathed doorway, on a mound
Of moss, was spread a feast of summer fruits,
Which nearer seen, seem'd refuse of a meal
By Angel tasted, or our Mother Eve;
For empty shells were scattered on the grass,
And grape stalks but half bare, and remnants more,
Sweet smelling, whose pure kinds I could not know.
Still was more plenty than the fabled horn
Thrice emptied could pour forth, at banqueting
For Proserpine return'd to her own fields,
Where the white heifers low. And appetite
More yearning than on earth I ever felt
Growing within, I ate deliciously;
And, after not long, thirsted, for thereby
Stood a cool vessel of transparent juice,
Sipp'd by the wander'd bee, the which I took,
And, pledging all the Mortals of the world,
And all the dead whose names are in our lips,
Drank. That full draught is parent of my theme.
No Asian poppy, nor Elixir fine
Of the soon fading jealous Caliphat;
No poison gender'd in close monkish cell

To thin the scarlet conclave of old men,
Could so have rapt unwilling life away.
Amongst the fragrant husks and berries crush'd,
Upon the grass I struggled hard against
The domineering potion; but in vain:
The cloudy swoon came on, and down I sunk
Like a Silenus on an antique vase.
How long I slumber'd 'tis a chance to guess.
When sense of life return'd, I started up
As if with wings; but the fair trees were gone,
The mossy mound and arbour were no more;
I look'd around upon the carved sides
Of an old sanctuary with roof august,
Builded so high, it seem'd that filmed clouds
Might spread beneath, as o'er the stars of heaven;
So old the place was, I remembered none
The like upon the earth: what I had seen
Of grey Cathedrals, buttress'd walls, rent towers,
The superannuations of sunk realms,
Or Nature's Rocks toil'd hard in waves and winds,
Seem'd but the faulture of decrepit things
To that eternal domed monument.
Upon the marble at my feet there lay
Store of strange vessels, and large draperies,
Which needs had been of dyed asbestos wove,
Or in that place the moth could not corrupt,
So white the linen; so, in some, distinct
Ran imageries from a sombre loom.
All in a mingled heap confus'd there lay
Robes, golden tongs, censer, and chafing dish,
Girdles, and chains, and holy jewelries —
    Turning from these with awe, once more I rais'd
My eyes to fathom the space every way;
The embossed roof, the silent massy range
Of columns north and south, ending in mist
Of nothing; then to Eastward, where black gates
Were shut against the sunrise evermore.
Then to the west I look'd, and saw far off

An Image, huge of feature as a cloud,
At level of whose feet an altar slept,
To be approach'd on either side by steps,
And marble balustrade, and patient travail
To count with toil the innumerable degrees.
Towards the altar sober-pac'd I went,
Repressing haste, as too unholy there;
And, coming nearer, saw beside the shrine
One minist'ring; and there arose a flame.
When in mid-May the sickening East Wind
Shifts sudden to the South, the small warm rain
Melts out the frozen incense from all flowers,
And fills the air with so much pleasant health
That even the dying man forgets his shroud;
Even so that lofty sacrificial fire,
Sending forth maian incense, spread around
Forgetfulness of everything but bliss,
And clouded all the altar with soft smoke,
From whose white fragrant curtains thus I heard
Language pronounc'd. 'If thou canst not ascend
These steps, die on that marble where thou art.
Thy flesh, near cousin to the common dust,
Will parch for lack of nutriment — thy bones
Will wither in few years, and vanish so
That not the quickest eye could find a grain
Of what thou now art on that pavement cold.
The sands of thy short life are spent this hour,
And no hand in the universe can turn
Thy hour glass, if these gummed leaves be burnt
Ere thou canst mount up these immortal steps.'
I heard, I look'd: two senses both at once
So fine, so subtle, felt the tyranny
Of that fierce threat, and the hard task proposed.
Prodigious seem'd the toil, the leaves were yet
Burning, — when suddenly a palsied chill
Struck from the paved level up my limbs,
And was ascending quick to put cold grasp
Upon those streams that pulse beside the throat:

I shriek'd; and the sharp anguish of my shriek
Stung my own ears — I strove hard to escape
The numbness; strove to gain the lowest step.
Slow, heavy, deadly was my pace: the cold
Grew stifling, suffocating, at the heart;
And when I clasp'd my hands I felt them not.
One minute before death, my iced foot touch'd
The lowest stair; and as it touch'd, life seem'd
To pour in at the toes: I mounted up,
As once fair Angels on a ladder flew
From the green turf to heaven. — 'Holy Power,'
Cried I, approaching near the horned shrine,
'What am I that should so be sav'd from death?
What am I that another death come not
To choak my utterance sacrilegious here?'
Then said the veiled shadow — 'Thou hast felt
What 'tis to die and live again before
Thy fated hour. That thou hadst power to do so
Is thy own safety; thou hast dated on
Thy doom.' 'High Prophetess,' said I, 'purge off
Benign, if so it please thee, my mind's film —'
'None can usurp this height,' returned that shade,
'But those to whom the miseries of the world
Are misery, and will not let them rest.
All else who find a haven in the world,
Where they may thoughtless sleep away their days,
If by a chance into this fane they come,
Rot on the pavement where thou rotted'st half. —'
'Are there not thousands in the world,' said I,
Encourag'd by the sooth voice of the shade,
'Who love their fellows even to the death;
Who feel the giant agony of the world;
And more, like slaves to poor humanity,
Labour for mortal good? I sure should see
Other men here: but I am here alone.'
'They whom thou spak'st of are no vision'ries,'
Rejoin'd that voice — 'they are no dreamers weak,
They seek no wonder but the human face;

No music but a happy-noted voice —
They come not here, they have no thought to come —
And thou art here, for thou art less than they —
What benefit canst thou do, or all thy tribe,
To the great world? Thou art a dreaming thing;
A fever of thyself — think of the Earth;
What bliss even in hope is there for thee?
What haven? every creature hath its home;
Every sole man hath days of joy and pain,
Whether his labours be sublime or low —
The pain alone; the joy alone; distinct:
Only the dreamer venoms all his days,
Bearing more woe than all his sins deserve.
Therefore, that happiness be somewhat shar'd,
Such things as thou art are admitted oft
Into like gardens thou didst pass erewhile,
And suffer'd in these Temples; for that cause
Thou standest safe beneath this statue's knees.'
'That I am favored for unworthiness,
By such propitious parley medicin'd
In sickness not ignoble, I rejoice,
Aye, and could weep for love of such award.'
So answer'd I, continuing, 'If it please,
Majestic shadow, tell me: sure not all
Those melodies sung into the world's ear
Are useless: sure a poet is a sage;
A humanist, Physician to all men.
That I am none I feel, as Vultures feel
They are no birds when Eagles are abroad.
What am I then? Thou spakest of my tribe:
What tribe?' — The tall shade veil'd in drooping white
Then spake, so much more earnest, that the breath
Mov'd the thin linen folds that drooping hung
About a golden censer from the hand
Pendent. — 'Art thou not of the dreamer tribe?
The poet and the dreamer are distinct,
Diverse, sheer opposite, antipodes.
The one pours out a balm upon the world,

The other vexes it.' Then shouted I
Spite of myself, and with a Pythia's spleen,
'Apollo! faded, farflown Apollo!
Where is thy misty pestilence to creep
Into the dwellings, thro' the door crannies,
Of all mock lyrists, large self-worshipers,
And careless Hectorers in proud bad verse.
Tho' I breathe death with them it will be life
To see them sprawl before me into graves.
Majestic shadow, tell me where I am,
Whose altar this; for whom this incense curls:
What Image this, whose face I cannot see,
For the broad marble knees; and who thou art,
Of accent feminine, so courteous.'
Then the tall shade, in drooping linens veil'd,
Spake out, so much more earnest, that her breath
Stirr'd the thin folds of gauze that drooping hung
About a golden censer from her hand
Pendent; and by her voice I knew she shed
Long-treasured tears. 'This temple sad and lone
Is all spar'd from the thunder of a war
Foughten long since by Giant Hierarchy
Against rebellion: this old Image here,
Whose carved features wrinkled as he fell,
Is Saturn's; I, Moneta, left supreme
Sole priestess of his desolation.' —
I had no words to answer; for my tongue,
Useless, could find about its roofed home
No syllable of a fit majesty
To make rejoinder to Moneta's mourn.
There was a silence while the altar's blaze
Was fainting for sweet food: I look'd thereon,
And on the paved floor, where nigh were pil'd
Faggots of cinnamon, and many heaps
Of other crisped spicewood — then again
I look'd upon the altar and its horns
Whiten'd with ashes, and its lang'rous flame,
And then upon the offerings again;

And so by turns — till sad Moneta cried,
'The sacrifice is done, but not the less,
Will I be kind to thee for thy goodwill.
My power, which to me is still a curse,
Shall be to thee a wonder; for the scenes
Still swooning vivid through my globed brain
With an electral changing misery
Thou shalt with those dull mortal eyes behold,
Free from all pain, if wonder pain thee not.'
As near as an immortal's sphered words
Could to a mother's soften, were these last:
But yet I had a terror of her robes,
And chiefly of the veils, that from her brow
Hung pale, and curtain'd her in mysteries
That made my heart too small to hold its blood.
This saw that Goddess, and with sacred hand
Parted the veils. Then saw I a wan face,
Not pin'd by human sorrows, but bright blanch'd
By an immortal sickness which kills not;
It works a constant change, which happy death
Can put no end to; deathwards progressing
To no death was that visage; it had pass'd
The lily and the snow; and beyond these
I must not think now, though I saw that face —
But for her eyes I should have fled away.
They held me back, with a benignant light,
Soft-mitigated by divinest lids
Half closed, and visionless entire they seem'd
Of all external things — they saw me not,
But in blank splendor beam'd like the mild moon,
Who comforts those she sees not, who knows not
What eyes are upward cast. As I had found
A grain of gold upon a mountain's side,
And twing'd with avarice strain'd out my eyes
To search its sullen entrails rich with ore,
So at the view of sad Moneta's brow,
I ached to see what things the hollow brain
Behind enwombed: what high tragedy

In the dark secret Chambers of her skull
Was acting, that could give so dread a stress
To her cold lips, and fill with such a light
Her planetary eyes; and touch her voice
With such a sorrow — 'Shade of Memory!'
Cried I, with act adorant at her feet,
'By all the gloom hung round thy fallen house,
By this last Temple, by the golden age,
By great Apollo, thy dear foster child,
And by thyself, forlorn divinity,
The pale Omega of a wither'd race,
Let me behold, according as thou said'st,
What in thy brain so ferments to and fro.' —

On Fame

How fever'd is the man, who cannot look
  Upon his mortal days with temperate blood,
Who vexes all the leaves of his life's book,
  And robs his fair name of its maidenhood;
It is as if the rose should pluck herself,
  Or the ripe plum finger its misty bloom,
As if a Naiad, like a meddling elf,
  Should darken her pure grot with muddy gloom:
But the rose leaves herself upon the briar,
  For winds to kiss and grateful bees to feed,
And the ripe plum still wears its dim attire,
  The undisturbed lake has crystal space;
  Why then should man, teasing the world for grace,
Spoil his salvation for a fierce miscreed?

To Sleep

O soft embalmer of the still midnight,
  Shutting, with careful fingers and benign,
Our gloom-pleas'd eyes, embower'd from the light,
  Enshaded in forgetfulness divine;
O soothest Sleep! if so it please thee, close,
  In midst of this thine hymn, my willing eyes,
Or wait the amen, ere thy poppy throws
  Around my bed its lulling charities;
  Then save me, or the passed day will shine
Upon my pillow, breeding many woes;
  Save me from curious conscience, that still lords
Its strength for darkness, burrowing like a mole;
  Turn the key deftly in the oiled wards,
And seal the hushed casket of my soul.

La Belle Dame Sans Merci

A BALLAD

I

O what can ail thee, knight-at-arms,
  Alone and palely loitering?
The sedge has wither'd from the lake,
  And no birds sing.

II

O what can ail thee, knight-at-arms,
  So haggard and so woe-begone?
The squirrel's granary is full,
  And the harvest's done.

III

I see a lilly on thy brow,
    With anguish moist and fever dew,
And on thy cheeks a fading rose
    Fast withereth too.

IV

I met a lady in the meads,
    Full beautiful — a faery's child,
Her hair was long, her foot was light,
    And her eyes were wild.

V

I made a garland for her head,
    And bracelets too, and fragrant zone;
She look'd at me as she did love,
    And made sweet moan.

VI

I set her on my pacing steed,
    And nothing else saw all day long,
For sidelong would she bend, and sing
    A faery's song.

VII

She found me roots of relish sweet,
    And honey wild, and manna dew,
And sure in language strange she said —
    'I love thee true'.

VIII

She took me to her elfin grot,
    And there she wept, and sigh'd full sore,
And there I shut her wild wild eyes
    With kisses four.

IX

And there she lulled me asleep,
   And there I dream'd — Ah! woe betide!
The latest dream I ever dream'd
   On the cold hill side.

X

I saw pale kings and princes too,
   Pale warriors, death-pale were they all;
They cried — 'La Belle Dame sans Merci
   Hath thee in thrall!'

XI

I saw their starved lips in the gloam,
   With horrid warning gaped wide,
And I awoke and found me here,
   On the cold hill's side.

XII

And this is why I sojourn here,
   Alone and palely loitering,
Though the sedge has wither'd from the lake,
   And no birds sing.

'Bright Star! Would I were steadfast'

Bright star! would I were steadfast as thou art —
   Not in lone splendour hung aloft the night
And watching, with eternal lids apart,
   Like nature's patient, sleepless Eremite,
The moving waters at their priestlike task
   Of pure ablution round earth's human shores,
Or gazing on the new soft fallen mask
   Of snow upon the mountains and the moors —

No — yet still steadfast, still unchangeable,
  Pillow'd upon my fair love's ripening breast,
To feel for ever its soft fall and swell,
  Awake for ever in a sweet unrest,
Still, still to hear her tender-taken breath,
And so live ever — or else swoon to death.

Stanzas

I

In a drear-nighted December,
    Too happy, happy tree,
Thy branches ne'er remember
    Their green felicity:
    The north cannot undo them,
    With a sleety whistle through them;
    Nor frozen thawings glue them
        From budding at the prime.

II

In a drear-nighted December,
    Too happy, happy brook,
Thy bubblings ne'er remember
    Apollo's summer look;
    But with a sweet forgetting,
    They stay their crystal fretting,
    Never, never petting
        About the frozen time.

Ah! would 'twere so with many
   A gentle girl and boy!
But were there ever any
   Writh'd not at passed joy?
The feel of not to feel it,
When there is none to heal it,
Nor numbed sense to steel it,
   Was never said in rhyme.

Index of First Lines

SOME FABER PAPER COVERED EDITIONS

A CHOICE OF BLAKE'S VERSE
Edited by Kathleen Raine

Miss Raine's selection is a splendid introduction—or reintroduction—to the poet of whom she writes: 'Seen in the light of his total achievement, our one national prophet emerges as a greater figure; whether we approach him as the prophet of the industrial revolution; as the reasoned opponent of the materialist philosophers; the predecessor of modern psychology, or the herald of a New Age; or, more simply, as the finest master of the metrics of the long line in English poetry'.

£0.50 *net*

A CHOICE OF SHELLEY'S VERSE
Edited by Stephen Spender

Stephen Spender, in the Introduction to his selection of Shelley's verse, provides a number of good reasons why Shelley 'remains a disturbing poetic presence even among modern poets who cannot accept his personality or his style'. He compares him with Goethe, and points out that 'deeper than the opinions and the neuroticism, there moves in Shelley that which Goethe anticipated from poetry: a world imagination, in which all pasts as well as the present, the landscapes of the several continents, and their civilizations, are contained'.

£0.50 *net*

A CHOICE OF SOUTHEY'S VERSE
Edited by Geoffrey Grigson

Southey is all too easy to parody. But, as Mr. Grigson points out in his sympathetic, judicious and persuasive introduction, one often feels that he is, even in poems mainly serious, 'stationing himself deliberately on the verge of self-parody . . . coupled with which is so often a clever touch of the morbid. . . .' This selection demonstrates convincingly that the least regarded of the Lake Poets wrote much that can still give pleasure.

£0.50 *net*

A CHOICE OF WORDSWORTH'S VERSE
Edited by R. S. Thomas

R. S. Thomas distinguishes in the Introduction to his selection of Wordsworth's poetry between the 'flat, rather featureless, often mawkish verse' with which the poet dutifully exemplified his theories of language, and that very great poetry 'soaring into the upper air of the spirit' with which Wordsworth transcended his theories and became a supreme poet of atmosphere.

£0.60 *net*